CW00672753

THE
CIRCULAR
ECONOMY
A WEALTH
OF FLOWS

KEN WEBSTER

Ellen MacArthur Foundation Publishing
The Sail Loft
42 Medina Road
Cowes
Isle of Wight PO31 7BX
United Kingdom
www.ellenmacarthurfoundation.org

Copyright © Ellen MacArthur Foundation 2015

Text copyright: Ellen MacArthur Foundation.

ISBN 978-0-9927784-2-2

First edition Ellen MacArthur Foundation Publishing

A catalogue record for this book is available from the British Library. All rights reserved. No part of this publication may be reproduced, stored in a retrieval system or transmitted, in any form or by any means, electronic, mechanical, photocopying, recording or otherwise, without the prior permission of the publishers. While every effort has been made to trace the owners of copyright material reproduced herein and secure permissions, the publishers would like to apologise for any omissions and will be pleased to incorporate missing acknowledgements in any future edition of this book.

Design and artwork by Graham Pritchard
Additional artwork: Sarah Churchill-Slough

Editors: Jocelyn Blériot, Craig Johnson and Ruth Sheppard

Copy editors: Caroline Walker and Mimi Quaife

Printed by Seacourt using 100% renewable energy-the world's first zero waste printer.

Printed on revive 100 Offset a recycled grade containing 100% post consumer waste and manufactured at a mill accredited with ISO14001 environmental management standard. The pulp used in this product is bleached using a Totally Chlorine Free process (TCF).

© Ken Webster 2015

Foreword

"What is our goal?" was the question I asked myself a lot in the period building up to the creation of the Ellen MacArthur Foundation. There was so much out there, but so much was about efficiency and buying ourselves time. Deep inside I had an uneasy feeling that incremental change wasn't going to work in an economy which was driven by using resources in a linear way.

I repeatedly felt like something wasn't right as I could only see part of the picture - that was until I met Ken Webster. Over 20 years he had been carefully inserting the pieces in the puzzle to build it until he understood it, reaching the point where he could see the economy running as a system. My inquisitive mind found immediate answers and great excitement in his work. He'd connected complementary schools of thought and shaped a coherent framework which, when applied to the economy, provided a sense of direction.

It was perhaps no surprise that just weeks after our first meeting Ken joined the original small team with which we launched the Ellen MacArthur Foundation.

"The Circular Economy: a Wealth of Flows" elaborates on the fundamental ideas that structure the circular economy and helps def ine the concept of a regenerative model, able to decouple economic development from the consumption of finite resources.

Crucially, Ken's understanding of framing and his ability to consistently refer to the 'big picture' allows him to break down silos and to provide a comprehensive narrative that addresses a variety of issues including societal implications, the role of finance, regenerative agriculture and education - to name but a few.

The circular economy gives us the opportunity to build a system that can run in the long term, and the time is right for it to reach scale, Ken's book argues... Big ideas don't simply pop up in a vacuum, and when real system-changing perspectives meet the right context, the resulting wave of transformation can seldom be resisted.

Ellen MacArthur

"Everything that needs to be said has already been said. But since no one was listening, everything must be said again. "
André Gide

Photo: Jocelyn Blériot

INTRODUCTION

"When you run out of red, use blue!" Pablo Picasso

Power, it is said, resides in the creation and maintenance of scarcity. The study of scarcity apparently belongs to economics, which claims that humankind's wants are limitless and its resources finite. It seems there will always be disappointment.

Mainstream Economics 101 assumes we are selfish, perfectly calculating about our wants, and rational decision makers. To the best operators go the prizes, it's a competitive world out there and markets – places and spaces where buyers and sellers meet and prices are determined – provide the best mechanism for allocating resources. Through the operation of markets the most *efficient* outcome – the lowest cost and best value – can be enjoyed all round. It creates just enough surplus which in turn allows for new investment and economic growth. An individual's choices benefit the economy as a whole: self-interest becomes the general interest. And that which may be placed outside the market, like forms of welfare, education and infrastructure, can then be afforded.

As a palliative to the story of disappointment is the story of economic growth which paradoxically is assumed to be limitless, based on new technologies, new sources of cheap energy and disruptive innovation, thus offering a promise of better times for all. 'A rising tide floats all boats', it is said, 'eventually'. It sounds so much better than wealth 'trickling down'.

In a roundabout way this caricature of an economy and of how humans really make decisions sort of worked as a story. For 150 years, from around 1830, rising living standards in the West, decade upon decade, showed the broad benefits of what is very much an economic machine which takes in resources, especially cheap energy and materials, and uses them to create and feed a mass production and consumption (and throwaway) society.

A linear economy, with its kickstarting money cycle, is massively wasteful of both raw materials and finished products. Elements and consequences outside the money-valued cycle are costs loaded onto the environment and society at large. The solution to this downside is the idea that increasing economic growth would allow enough surplus to clean up the mess and heal the sick - the cure was hiding inside the problem. Like medicine, economic growth might taste a bit rough but the outcome is, apparently, admirable.

This general story is very much still current. Since many in developed countries would like to extend a modern world to those not yet benefitting, it might seem mischievous to suggest another story, but this book is based on exactly that. Imagine the economy as circular, a place where 'roundput' not 'throughput' dominates, where everything is food for the cycles of materials, where resources are used but not used up, where the feedback – it is built on feedback – restores capital and enables additional flows of goods and services. In such a circular economy money and finance, a key information flow, is constantly recirculated and reaches all parts of the economy to facilitate exchange. It is a better story because it engages with the changing facts on the ground – the exhaustion of cheap energy, easy-to-get minerals, materials and productive credit.

It also closely reflects recent trends and developments in scientific thinking. The economy, we are told by the likes of Paul Ormerod[1] and Eric Beinhocker,[2] is a complex adaptive system – much more a metabolism than a machine. It is also a story about the possibilities of abundance, of meeting people's needs by designing out waste and recreating the kind of elegant abundance so evident in living systems. That is economic growth, but not as we define it today. It has much more in it about a quality of life than mere throughput; again it's the connections, the relationships not the stuff that is the focus.

Simple ————————————————
Equilibrium ————————————
Linear ——————————————————
Mechanistic ————————————
Efficient ——————————————
Predictive ————————————————
Independent ——————————————
Individual ability ——————————
Rational calculator ——————————
Selfish ——————————————————
Win-lose ————————————————
Competition ——————————————

The reasoning is practical at its heart: that the constellation of factors which made a linear throughput economy so successful, for so many and for so long (at considerable cost to others and the general fabric of environment it has to be said) has shifted. It's simply not doing what it has hitherto always promised. To add to this, science has indeed moved on a long way from the mechanistic discipline that historically has informed a mechanistic view of economics and of the way humans think and behave. The assumptions underlying the old narrative have begun to fall away as well (see below).

→ **Complex**
→ **Disequilibrium**
→ **Non-linear**
→ **Behavioural**
→ **Effective**
→ **Adaptive**
→ **Interdependent**
→ **Group diversity**
→ **Irrational approximators**
→ **Strongly reciprocal**
→ **Win-win or lose-lose**
→ **Cooperation**

The 21st century is yielding a second Enlightenment. The narrative it offers about what makes us tick, individually and collectively, is infinitely more sophisticated than we previously thought. Across many fields the above changes have occurred since the 1960s.

Adapted from Hanauer and Liu[3]

The old story increasingly doesn't work and it's no longer a convincing narrative.

Some people really don't like stories or narratives about the economy, or pretend that they simply don't need one: all they want to do is find the business opportunity therein, see which way the wind is blowing and take advantage. One of the advantages of a circular economy is that it is perfectly possible to work this way, starting from today, although like all systems it will be far more successful if the various incentives, regulations, tax codes and other enablers are pointing in the same direction. After all, paddling upstream can be tiresome.

The point is one does not need a change of values to get involved. In discussing his recent book *Reinventing Fire* – a sophisticated approach to moving away from a fossil fuel-dominated economy[4] – Amory Lovins claims that:

"Whether you care most about profits and jobs and competitive advantage or national security, or environmental stewardship and climate protection and public health, *Reinventing Fire* makes sense and makes money."

Amory Lovins is the founder of Rocky Mountain Institute (RMI) in Colorado, USA. He is keen on the abundance theme and has even trade-marked 'Abundance by Design'. A major point in *Reinventing Fire* is that a shift to optimising the whole system, rather than focussing on a part, brings a series of reinforcing benefits – a spiral or 'upcycle' as William McDonough and Michael Braungart say.

In *Natural Capitalism*,[5] Amory Lovins, Hunter Lovins and Paul Hawken explore how this abundance can be built by implementing four reinforcing shifts, not just one, but all four, to create a positive cycle. In this book all four are likewise considered part of a circular economy.

Shift 1: implement resource efficiency – actually 'radical resource efficiency' not the few per cent kind from the picking of a few low-hanging fruits around the business.

Resource efficiency is a big favourite, as we shall see: design to recover materials; design for disassembly; design for cleaner material flows and shared standards; and design for remanufacturing. They can all cut energy use, maintain product quality and cut waste.

But the other three shifts are needed too, if the aim is a win-win 'upcycle'. This sense of the whole system being optimised sets a circular economy aside from a lot of waste minimisation approaches which do not question the throughput character of the economy and just seek to ameliorate its effects and carve out a little extra on the bottom line. Simple recycling, for example, does not challenge a throughput economy because it is always incomplete and many applications are for low-value, fast-cycle items with appreciable material leakages.

WHY RESOURCE EFFICIENCY IS NOT ENOUGH

"

Without a fundamental rethinking of the structure and the reward system of commerce, narrowly focused eco-efficiency could be a disaster for the environment by overwhelming resource savings with even larger growth in the production of the wrong products, produced by the wrong processes, from the wrong materials, in the wrong place, at the wrong scale, and delivered using the wrong business models. With so many wrongs outweighing one right, more efficient production by itself could become not the servant but the enemy of a durable economy. Reconciling ecological with economic goals requires not just eco-efficiency alone, but also three additional principles, all interdependent and mutually reinforcing. Only that combination of all four principles can yield the full benefits and the logical consistency of natural capitalism.[6]
Amory Lovins et al., *Natural Capitalism: Creating the Next Industrial Revolution* (1999)

"

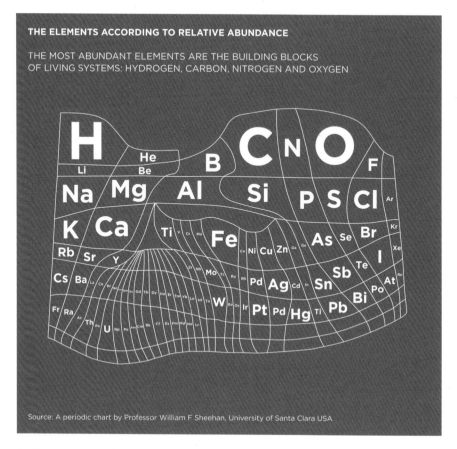

THE ELEMENTS ACCORDING TO RELATIVE ABUNDANCE

THE MOST ABUNDANT ELEMENTS ARE THE BUILDING BLOCKS
OF LIVING SYSTEMS: HYDROGEN, CARBON, NITROGEN AND OXYGEN

Source: A periodic chart by Professor William F Sheehan, University of Santa Clara USA

Shift 2: move to biomimetic modes of production. Use the 'everything is food' notion to redesign, and design out waste. Some commentators like Janine Benyus advance an overall shift to a largely 'bio based' materials economy, using living systems as 'model, mentor and measure'.

Shift 3: move to providing services rather than goods. There are various elements to this – the performance economy, other product-service systems and more recently the explosion of interest in how information technology can furnish access to products and assets for short periods of time with low transaction costs. ZipCar, Lyft and AirBnB are examples.

Shift 4: reinvest in natural capital. To create additional flows of materials and energy from rebuilt or restored/maintained capital stocks over time. To support diversity and hence creativity and resilience (two vital functions). Others add 'social capital,' the ability of individuals and communities to add value in what they do for each other – this is an oft-cited feature of the so-called 'sharing economy.'

McDonough and Braungart's 'cradle to cradle', as a design philosophy – the seminal book of the same name is at the heart of a circular economy – is also a very practical approach to improving quality, from urban planning to products and materials science. Their core principles again emphasise the big picture and draw insights from living systems for their strength.

Key 'cradle to cradle' principles include:
• All materials flow in one of two cycles: biological (can be safely decomposed through the biosphere) or technical (non biodegradable, kept at high quality and away from the biosphere in their own industrial cycle)
• Everything is food (sometimes described as waste = food)
• Shift towards renewables
• Celebrate diversity (in part as a source of creativity and resilience in systems)

Hundreds of products have been redesigned to reflect a cradle to cradle approach,[7] and where it succeeds the advantage is not only manifest in the returns to the business but also more widely.

This notion 'more widely' is another important element of a circular economy. It is about the economy writ large and, to return to the overall story, is about an economy that will work long term and add, not detract, from social and environmental capital and flows. It does this by being an effective circulatory system, optimised, yet dynamic. The prosperity principle behind it is 'we're all better off when we are all better off'[8], or, to use living systems insights, 'healthy trees are found in healthy forests'.

Because a circular economy is a dynamic system and inclusive, it is an economy which includes flows of resources (energy and materials), and information, for example prices (as messages), and money and financial flows. An economy is too often seen as only the exchange of monetised goods and services through markets. This is too narrow for a circular economy, although there are clear advantages in even those terms to those with the better business models.

A circular economy is one that is restorative by design, and which aims to keep products, components and materials at their highest utility and value, at all times.

1 Circular economy is a global economic model that decouples economic growth and development from the consumption of finite resources;

2 Distinguishes between and separates technical and biological materials, keeping them at their highest value at all times.

3 Focuses on effective design and use of materials to optimise their flow and maintain or increase technical and natural resource stocks;

4 Provides new opportunities for innovation across fields such as product design, service and business models, food, farming, biological feedstocks and products;

5 Establishes a framework and building blocks for a resilient system able to work in the longer term.

Source: Ellen MacArthur Foundation

Photo: Thinkstock

The linear economy is the central flow downwards on the diagram opposite. The feedback loops of a circular economy are identified following the convention of biological and technical materials flows (coloured green and blue respectively).

Here then is the starting point but also the conclusion. What follows in this book is an elaboration of what a circular economy might mean for some of the key relationships in an economy. There are several chapters which make the business case, including a chapter from Walter Stahel, the instigator of the cradle to cradle concept at the end of the 1970s. The book is not comprehensive in the strict sense, as the boundaries of a circular economy are not defined, nor are they ever likely to be. It is more of an exploration and reiteration of the salient characteristics; after all – to pick up on Picasso's aphorism at the start of the introduction – learning to paint in blue when you want red and it's just run out is quite a challenge. But it's more a challenge to the imagination than anything else. After all, Marcel Proust reminds us:

"The voyage of discovery lies not in seeking new horizons, but in seeing with new eyes."

The circular economy – an industrial system that is restorative by design

Imagine the economy as circular, a place where 'roundput' not 'throughput' dominates, where everything is food for the cycles of materials, where resources are used but not used up, where the feedback – it is built on feedback – restores capital and enables additional flows of goods and services.

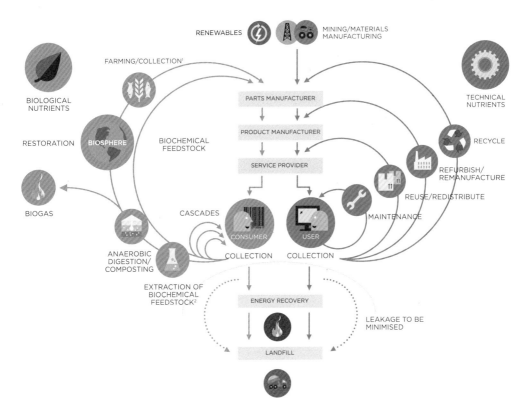

Diagram as found in the report Towards a Circular Economy by the Ellen MacArthur Foundation created with the support of McKinsey and Company.

1 Hunting and fishing
2 Can take both post-harvest and post-consumer waste as an input
SOURCE: Ellen MacArthur Foundation - Adapted from the Cradle to Cradle Design Protocol by Braungart & McDonough

A circular economy summarised

An economy – built on the endless flow of energy from the sun **(energy in surplus)** – which transforms materials into useful goods and services endlessly **(waste = food)**.

It **builds capital** and maintains it. Money is alchemical: it is information which stimulates and co-ordinates the exchange of all things at all levels and, as if by magic, our *prima materia* is transformed **(money as a medium of exchange)**. To do this, **prices act as messages** and – just as materials need to flow cleanly, uncontaminated, to become food for new cycles – prices need to **reflect the full costs** to do their job.

Like all living systems, a circular economy is dynamic but adaptive and, if enduring, it will be **effective**, neither courting disaster by over-extending efficiency **(brittleness)** or becoming too resistant to change **(stagnation)**.

It celebrates diversity – of scale, culture, place, connection and time – because a dynamic system is full of change, by definition. And thriving in such an environment requires diversity as a fount of **creative adaption**, a means of **resilience**, a source of redundancy or back-up.

A circular economy is led by **business for a profit** within the 'rules of the game' decided by **an active citizenship in a flourishing democracy**.

**A collection of key relationships –
or the story within the story**

Energy in surplus is a precondition, eventually
mostly renewables (using flows not stocks)

Waste = food (everything is 'food'). An upcycle,
it (re)**builds** natural and social **capital and
maintains it**

Money as a medium of exchange (as credit,
it leads the cycle)

Markets work if **prices act as messages** and
reflect the full costs

Effective flows not just efficient (optimise the
whole not the part)

Celebrates diversity for reasons of **creativity**
and **resilience** (to keep a dynamic system 'up'
but adaptive)

Led by business for a profit but within rules set by
an active citizenship in a flourishing democracy.
Democracy probably requires relative abundance
not scarcity in order to thrive.

" Thinking in systems and cycles, we become metabolists ""

Gunter Pauli

At the moment we live in an economy which is overwhelmingly linear. It is a take-make-and-dispose system powered by fossil fuels. It is like a machine: the bigger it is and the faster it runs, the more efficiently it runs, and the more it produces – so long as there are resources to transform and sinks for the wastes, credit for investment and enough economic growth to pay for it all. That is what has created the modern world and its comforts. That is also why we need to think it through afresh. Resources are expensive and getting more so, waste sinks are full, credit limited and growth stumbling. Meanwhile, three billion new middle-class consumers are waiting in the wings, expectantly.

❝ If the machine inspired the industrial age, the image of the living system may inspire a genuine postindustrial age. ❞

Peter Senge et al *in Sloan Management Review*

Wood glue based on protein chemistry of blue mussel

PureBond developed its non-formaldehyde wood glue modelled on the protein chemistry of the blue mussel's byssus threads, which keep the mussel attached to wave-battered rocks. This glue is less toxic for building occupants than formaldehyde glues.

Water mixer uses centripetal spiral modelled on the nautilus shell

The PAX Water Mixer uses propeller technology based on the centripetal spiral, a recurrent form in nature (e.g. nautilus shell), to more efficiently maintain drinking water safety. The system uses efficiencies of fluid flow to mix water in storage tanks, eliminating stratification to ensure healthy water quality.

Wireless energy management system based on bees' 'swarm logic'

REGEN's EnviroGrid™ is a system that can be installed quickly and can cut a property owner's electric costs by 5-10% or more.

Carpet design inspired by random patterns on forest floor

Interface plc has created innovative carpet tiles that feature a random, non-directional pattern and gradations of colours. These design features allow for individual tile replacement without worrying about matching patterns, thereby saving materials, waste, and money.

Source of the biomimicry case studies: The Biomimicry 3.8 Institute

1 ALL THE FLOWS, HISTORY TOO

There is an arc to change, a time when often disparate forces align and the long-mooted but hesitant becomes possible, or indeed necessary. It is reasonable to start in many places and many times to begin to track these forces – say the USA and Europe at the end of the post-war boom, or the shock of the fall of the Berlin Wall (and the end to one form of bipolar political world), or perhaps the birth of the computer age and the emergence of a truly global economy. Conventionally, however, the story starts with a reminder about materials and energy use, seeing as how the economy is embedded in materials, energy and information flows. That truism, that passing assumption is important. At one stage, at the turn of the 20th century, the economy became 'disconnected' from its resource base and it was assumed that it was about a circular flow of income and an accumulation of wealth driven by the idealised decision-making of individuals and businesses seeking maximum 'utility' or satisfaction from moment to moment – the neoclassical consensus. To get a representation of what this implies, take a look at the diagram opposite, and imagine the two elements highlighted (in outer blue circles) are out of the equation – energy was boundless and cheap, materials endless if enough energy, technology and human ingenuity was applied. Money was the economy's measure, the arbiter too of what was included, and therefore important, or excluded, and not important.

Natural and social capital, the reservoirs of resources for production became an incidental part of the economic playbook rather than the economy being nested within environment and what society demanded of the economy.

It's best to lay this narrow focus to one side early on – the economy discussed in this book is assumed to have an intimate connection with energy and 'stuff' and how it all flows. The economy is embedded. The inescapable laws of thermodynamics apply to it as much as anything else. It feels rather strange having to make this point, but the level of disconnection that has been reached in our mental representation of the economic system is such that it is necessary to emphasise it.

FLOWS WITHIN AN ECONOMY

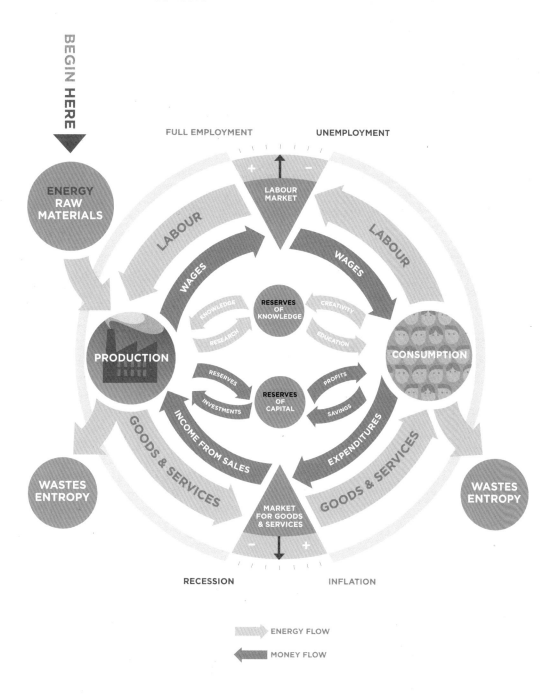

Adapted from: Joël de Rosnay, *The Macroscope* (1979)

We may be close to a time of pervasive change: high but volatile materials prices are emerging that are associated with declining materials accessibility, ore concentration, or both. These material prices are also part of a long business cycle too, one which left many raw materials at the bottom of a long decline in prices over the entire 20th century. It affected energy too; oil was around USD 15 a barrel in 1999. Ugo Bardi has argued that the availability and price of energy is the key to whether ores and deposits are worked. Mining takes between 5% and 10% of global energy production.[1] The diagram opposite captures some of the changes.

Coupled to these materials trends is rising demand from the new middle classes – defined as those earning between USD 10 and USD 100 a day – and a world population that is still rising (but at a declining rate). Demand for water is becoming a pivot for geopolitical disputes, and groundwater, 'fossil' water supplies in many cases (water that has taken thousands of years to filter down), is depleting rapidly.

Other measures of natural capital show declines: fisheries' stocks, forests, and significantly soil losses, which amount to nearly 4 tonnes per person per year.[2] All of these tightening natural resource supply chains invite speculative activity, leading to very damaging volatility and turning already difficult trading for manufacturers, who need to plan ahead, into potential mayhem. It is easy to see that this emerging configuration leads to short-termism, and that, as a result, the current global economy can arguably be seen as not much more than a race for the remaining resources.

There are the wastes too, and the toxicity, a panoply of endocrine disruption at one end to the dismal life-shortening smogs of a Mexico City, Tehran or Beijing at another. The surplus of carbon in the atmosphere as carbon dioxide is disrupting weather patterns and crop yields, for example, and bringing additional extreme weather events and rapid changes in the ice caps.

Grouping several significant trends, the *New Scientist* has published this graphic.[3] While it presents a somewhat disturbing view of our world, it can also prompt the thought that we are looking at big picture systems-wide change here. That is where the solutions will also be found.

A few illustrations here will serve to reinforce the point and the detail can be found in any number of what has become a cascade of books and information in recent years, among them *Bankrupting Nature*, by Anders Wijkman and Johan Rockström, *The Future,* by Al Gore, and the Worldwatch Institute series *State of the World and Vital Signs.*[4]

**SHARP PRICE INCREASES IN COMMODITIES SINCE 2000 HAVE ERASED
ALL THE REAL PRICE DECLINES OF THE 20TH CENTURY**

MCKINSEY COMMODITY PRICE INDEX (YEARS 1999-2001=100)

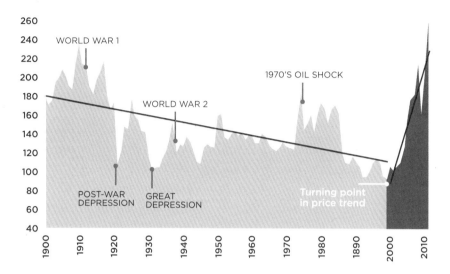

ALL TOGETHER NOW

● NORTHERN HEMISPHERE
   AVERAGE SURFACE
   TEMPERATURE

● POPULATION

● CO_2 CONCENTRATION

● GDP

● WATER USE

● PAPER CONSUMPTION

● LOSS OF TROPICAL
   RAINFOREST AND
   WOODLAND

● MOTOR VEHICLES

● OZONE DEPLETION

● FOREIGN INVESTMENT

● FISHERIES EXPLOITED

● SPECIES EXTINCTION

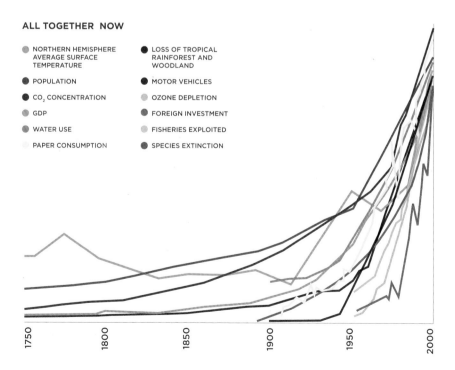

Adapted from: *New Scientist* (October 19th, 2008).

10-YEAR AVERAGE ANNUAL GROWTH IN CROP YIELDS

STRESS IN THE AGRICULTURAL AREA: FALLING
INCREASES IN CROP YIELDS MATCHED WITH
POPULATION GROWTH.

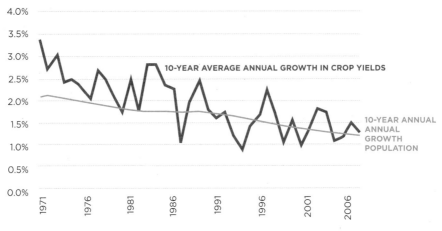

Source: FAO, 2009

RECOVERABLE COPPER ORE YIELD GRADE

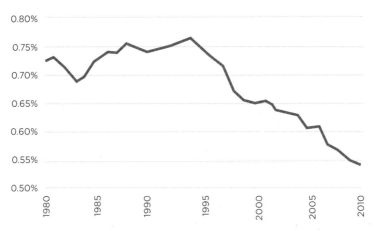

Source: Barclays Capital

The century-long trend for falling materials prices noted earlier has been reversed since the year 2002 (see upper graph page 31). Although volatile, the analysts at GMO, led by Jeremy Grantham, are confident that this trend is not a random artefact, nor one likely to be overwritten by investment or the upswing of the commodities cycle as high prices open up new mining ventures.[5]

One example is the concentration of ore in mining operations. Copper is the commodity illustrated in the graphic opposite. Ore concentrations continue to fall prompting more expenditure, especially in innovations in material recovery and the need for high and rising prices to compensate.[6]

Adding to this are the coming resource shocks from China and India and no doubt Russia, Brazil and South Africa (the so-called BRICS nations) so that the upward trend looks to be continuous, if volatile (speculators are at work in these and all 'tight' markets and the Great Recession put downward pressure on prices). McKinsey & Company characterised this shock by drawing out the doubling times for GDP for various nations and their populations. The realisation that a country as populous as China is doubling its economy nearly every ten years inevitably provokes a certain troublesome feeling around materials and resources. It is not just the material costs which are at stake. In both this and the energy markets the question of security of supply looms large. Already China, with almost all of the production of rare earth metals in its control – vital to the electronics and renewables industries – has cut supply on more than one occasion in defiance of World Trade Organisation (WTO) rules.

Energy is a much disputed arena, especially since the natural gas 'fracking' boom and the exploitation of 'tight' oil (shale oil) in the USA have received a great deal of publicity. It might be best to tackle this from a longer-term perspective. Here is a graphic (page 34) of the timing and size of discoveries of oil and their exploitation, followed by some comments (page 35) on the key issues relating to oil supply.

DISCOVERIES V EXPLOITATION

BILLION BARRELS OF
OIL PER YEAR (GB/A)

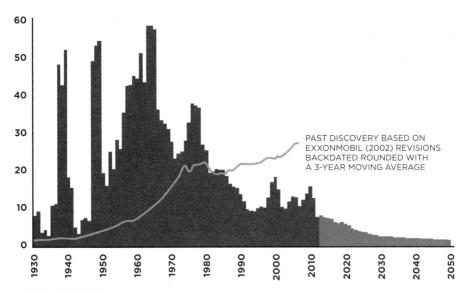

PAST DISCOVERY BASED ON
EXXONMOBIL (2002) REVISIONS
BACKDATED ROUNDED WITH
A 3-YEAR MOVING AVERAGE

■ PAST DISCOVERY
■ FUTURE DISCOVERY
— PRODUCTION

Adapted from: Colin Campbell, ASPO, Ireland

It's not what is in the earth nor even what is in the known
reserves (the tank). Rather, it's about the flow (the size
of the tap), the amount of energy needed to actually
extract the oil or gas and the price in terms of dollars
of the energy used to extract the oil or gas. Oil may
become unaffordable before it becomes really scarce.

An extract from an interview with Chris Nelder, an energy analyst and consultant in the *Washington Post*:

In 2005, we reached 73 million barrels per day. Then, to increase production beyond that, the world had to double spending on oil production. In 2012, we're now spending USD 600 billion. The price of oil has tripled. And yet, for all that additional expenditure, we've only raised production 3 percent to 75 million barrels per day [since 2005].

At some point, you wind up investing so much energy to produce more energy that you start losing the race. It becomes non-useful or ineffective to keep trying to produce more energy.

And there's a turning point on this – it's called the 'the net energy cliff'. When the ratio of energy output to energy input gets down to about 6 to 1, then you fall off this cliff, and it's just not worth doing. In the early days of oil production, that ratio was about 100 to 1.[7] Globally, right now, it's approaching 11 to 1. And it's even lower for some newer sources. The return on investment for heavy oil from the Kern River field in California is about 4 to 1.

The point is that the net energy available to society has been declining radically. If you want to run a society, your net energy for oil production has to be at least 5 to 1. And if you want to run a modern complex society, with televisions, iPads, highly advanced medicine, etc., then you probably need an Energy Return On Investment (EROI) closer to 10 to 1. So it's reaching the point where we're in the danger zone.

The upshot is that we need to prepare for the day when oil is going to leave us. The sooner we commit to an energy transition, to renewable energy, the better off we'll be in every respect. You can make that argument just on the basis of production rates and price. And that's not even considering carbon emissions and climate change, which is another great reason. Let alone what oil is doing to the global economy.

Chris Nelder[8]

Our current linear economy is substantially built on the premise of the surplus which cheap energy provides. Research by James Murray and Jim Hansen[9] points to International Monetary Fund (IMF) data proving a historically "strong correlation between global economic growth (measured by an average of gross domestic product (GDP)) and oil production." They note that out of eleven recessions in the United States since World War 2, ten were preceded by oil price spikes.

To many businesses these energy and materials concerns demand a response, since any business built on cheap energy and materials and mass consumption may well struggle if materials and energy are no longer cheap. Since the financial collapse of 2007/8 and the bumpy fitful state of the economy which has followed, it is clear that the last of the trinity – credit for consumption – is also deeply problematic for business. The debt overhang – the need to repay debts and the effect that this has on money available for other things like consumer purchases – is cramping both the demand for, and supply of, credit to Main Street.

As noted earlier, the economy is not only embedded in these energy and materials flows; we must also consider information flows through the systems. There is change now of the most profound kind associated with information technology. Changes include the rise in labour productivity – so much more can be produced with less in ever more automated factories and streamlined distribution systems (see Chapter 8). Information technology has also opened up new possibilities and markets, whether for dairy farmers in India bypassing the middlemen, or the eBay phenomenon, or the connectivity of the world resulting from the Internet and mobile telephony – there are now more mobile phones than conventional toilets. Information technology allows access to information and each other: it has already completely changed the financial industry and the music and creative industries, and transformed travel – everyone now being their own travel agent – and is beginning to disrupt education and training in an equally profound way.

None of these IT trends might make the flow of materials and energy more benign, in fact they could even worsen the situation with more poorly designed products circulating ever more widely and quickly.

Everywhere information technology can be applied to assets (financial products of course but also infrastructure, houses, vehicles, tools, materials, people) and the tracking of assets. With the creation of an 'internet of things', when the appliances communicate with each other and associated energy systems, there follows what can only be described as seismic shifts in the business models of a technical civilisation. Already huge corporations have grown up using IT to manage assets of all kinds.

Information technology potentially allows the tools of the economy, the medium- and long-life durable products, to become the basis for a market in the services they provide, rather than just selling the product itself. With appropriate maintenance, value is added by product life extension; after that, the materials can be recovered as valuable components and sub-assemblies, which can, in turn, be refurbished and reused and improved. Information technology allows easy administration and the billing for a thousand small transactions. It even allows the creation of designer currencies to reach the parts of the economy not served by the conventional currency monocultures (see Chapter 6).

The circular economy, if it is to come, will be the product of many forces: the realities of materials and energy supply and price interactions; the growth of demand worldwide from new consumers; and the pressures of uncosted externalities on societies and governments and the economy – there is no 'away' for waste to go. But arguably the central catalyst will be the possibilities that information technology offers for business models which will stimulate entrepreneur and established business alike and transform our relationships with the industrial economy.

The economy, however, is not a shiny object, made only of energy, materials, information and knowledge. It is also part of a system with its own history, constraints and consequences. Where we are now needs understanding more broadly and the next chapter revisits the evolution of the global economy since World War 2 and points out more of the challenges which need to be overcome before a circular economy can emerge.

Photo: Jocelyn Blériot

2 THE NECESSITY OF A CIRCULAR ECONOMY?

❝ All things happen through strife and necessity ❞
Heraclitus (c600 BC)

What if a circular economy went from being a promising innovation platform for entrepreneurs and established businesses looking for new profit streams in turbulent times to the category of necessity?

Heraclitus, the first philosopher of change, had it right. There is the struggle, there is what we choose, and there is a bigger necessity that we cannot resist. Throwing a ball higher than someone else is the 'strife' and seeing all of these balls fall under gravity is the necessity.

This chapter makes the case for the necessity of a circular economy from an historical perspective. It's a look at the recent history of the Western economies and some of the consequences of the existing economic arrangements, as well as what may be emerging as a result.

Something quite profound happened in the mid to late 1970s. The average wage for employees lost touch with economic growth. Every decade for the previous 150 years had seen rising living standards in the USA, and it was much the same across Europe. Wages, now stagnated as a proportion of the economic pie and inflation-adjusted, have not risen significantly since. Profitability increased markedly across the board however, as productivity kept rising, as did inequality of income. Economic growth has largely become jobless growth backfilled with increasing numbers of part-time, short-contract and low-paid workers. These workers do not make confident consumers.

GROWTH OF REAL HOURLY COMPENSATION

PRODUCTION/NONSUPERVISORY WORKERS
AND PRODUCTIVITY 1948-2011

CUMULATIVE PERCENT CHANGE SINCE 1948

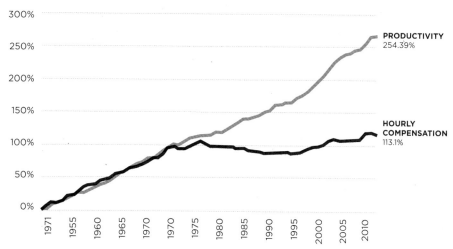

Source: Paul Krugman

HOUSEHOLD MORTGAGE AND CONSUMER DEBT

HOUSEHOLD DEBT/INCOME
RATIO IS STILL EXTREMELY HIGH

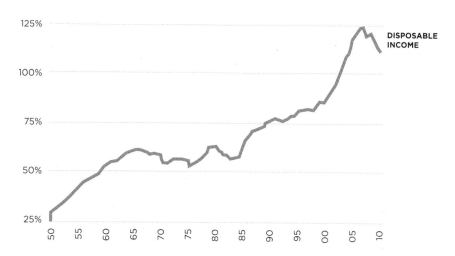

Source: Federal Reserve Board, Department of Commerce

There are several reasons for this wage stagnation, including: offshoring; increasing labour productivity; the presence of many more women in the labour force; more part-time workers; new technologies – especially the lead-up to the digital revolution; deregulation and growth of the financial sector; and the breakdown of the social contract – especially after the end of the Cold War in the mid to late 1980s. The focus for now is on the proportions of the economic pie and where they go.

Sufficient wages overall, however, are needed to buy all the products being produced and if there are more goods but less spending power, even if cheaper goods arrive from abroad, it's a problem.

In recent times, credit has been needed to bridge the gap since wages did not suffice. It was a necessity if the economy was not to fall into recession and worse. The economy has two main modes: expansion and contraction, and each has its reinforcing feedback mechanisms. Growth soon switches into its evil twin if the flow of goods and services produced is out of balance with available purchasing power. Hence credit for, well, everyone as far as possible (see graph below for household debt trends). Credit provision also made sense as a way of using the additional profits from business very profitably. Mass production requires mass consumption, which in turn requires credit, both secured and unsecured, for producer and consumer. Several car companies, and GM is the prime example, had long used credit subsidiaries to supply consumers with the

DEBT DISTRIBUTION

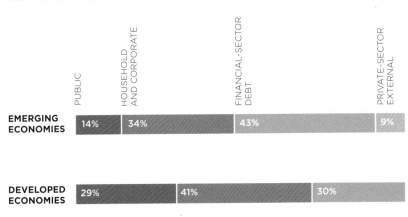

Source: ING/Th ll Street Journal

means to purchase the company's own cars. Very often, these 'banks' were far more profitable than the unit selling vehicles and extended their operations into real estate and insurance – at least until the financial crash of 2007–08.

Debt is a claim on future wealth. Debt therefore demands economic growth to meet the interest payments, if these payments are not to become an ever bigger part of the economic pie and prompt a downward spiral – less spending, less production, less work and so on.

Credit creation, if done prudently, requires some assets as collateral and classically this means property, usually real estate or stocks and shares or bonds. The expansion of credit tends to increase the price of these assets and there is a pressure upwards that can accelerate and lead to a bubble phenomenon. This happened in the USA several times after the 1980s – the Savings and Loans crisis, the stock market Internet stocks bubble of 1999, and finally the real estate bubble of 2003–08. With the collapse of the last, and despite the injection of more liquidity than the USA spent on World War 2, the Marshall Plan, Vietnam and the wars in the Middle East combined (see below), the USA and most other OECD economies remain relatively lifeless six years on – outside of stock markets and financials, unsurprisingly.

THE 2008 BAILOUT VERSUS OTHER LARGE US GOVERNMENT PROJECTS

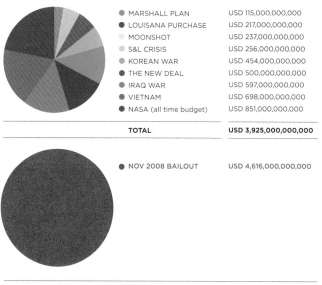

● MARSHALL PLAN	USD 115,000,000,000
● LOUISANA PURCHASE	USD 217,000,000,000
● MOONSHOT	USD 237,000,000,000
● S&L CRISIS	USD 256,000,000,000
● KOREAN WAR	USD 454,000,000,000
● THE NEW DEAL	USD 500,000,000,000
● IRAQ WAR	USD 597,000,000,000
● VIETNAM	USD 698,000,000,000
● NASA (all time budget)	USD 851,000,000,000
TOTAL	**USD 3,925,000,000,000**

● NOV 2008 BAILOUT	USD 4,616,000,000,000

Source: www.voltagecreative.com/blog

Asia is an exception to an extent, but signs of an overheated real-estate boom in China and slowing economic growth are present there as well. Growth has helped to fuel rising trend, but volatile, materials and energy prices. This added to the dampening effects on the economy of the fall off in credit. From a manufacturing perspective, Europe, the USA and Japan have saturated markets for cars and most categories of durable goods and, as a consequence, the market is little more than replacement.

Other social trends add to a worrying picture: increasingly ageing populations and rising unemployment – particularly among the under 25s – are calling on more public provision just as public funds are strained in the aftermath of rescuing the financial sector. The overhang of private

BOOSTING DEMAND BY CHANGING MINDSETS

In the 1930s, goods were not being sold in part because demand was low, work was not being done because wages could not be paid and firms went bust because profits disappeared. Not enough money and not enough spending.

A contributing factor was that many goods lasted a long while, could be repaired, or were seen as adequate. The 1930s depression was only finally overcome by the arrival of preparations for war and the forced spending by government that this brought. However manufacturers had also learnt some valuable lessons about protecting their businesses. Customers had to be persuaded that more was better and 'new' stuff was better than old; that borrowing money was morally acceptable and modern, while conversely renting was always inferior to owning. Also that holding onto goods had a downside – they needed repair, and this was increasingly not a route which should be open to the user, but only to the specialist.

Having absorbed these lessons from the 1930s consumer spending was encouraged and the flow of resources and manufactures accelerated and a concomitant flow of waste materials accumulated rapidly.

Businesses increasingly designed for much shorter product lifecycles. Lightbulbs were an early example, guaranteed to last 1,000 hours, or little more in the 1930s, compared to around 2,500 hours a few years before. Result: more sales, which suited the mass production line and nicely limited the liability of the manufacturer for the reliability and of course the onward destination of the product.

AGE-RELATED EXPENDITURE IN THE EUROPEAN UNION AS % OF GDP, % OF GDP

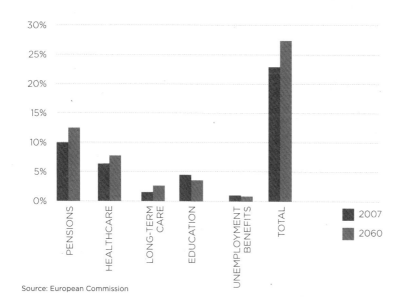

Source: European Commission

debt (household, corporate and financial) is huge and the public sector debt, while smaller, is still significant. The debt in the private sector means that income is increasingly going to paying it down and thus not to new consumption or investment in productive goods. In the public sector high debt levels, particularly after 2008, also restrict expenditure or force public spending cuts, often described by the term 'austerity'.

The industrial era of prosperity began to move out of focus in the 1970s as productivity parted company with median wage levels and was shocked to a standstill in the year 2008. If this linear economy can be characterised as throughput- and efficiency-led, based on cheap energy and materials (substituting for labour), supported by easy credit – which was in turn held up by economic growth – then truly it has run out of steam.

We have surplus goods, surplus in that there is insufficient effective demand for these goods, leading to factories running under capacity, expensive energy, difficult credit conditions, and poor growth/stagnation. All this tends to undermine health, education, savings and pensions, and what remains of the weakening contract between state and society. Declining environmental conditions have been noted in the *New Scientist* graph in Chapter 1. For completeness, rising inequality, working to its own feedback-rich cycles, forms a potentially very disruptive but less discussed part of the mix.

"Factors affecting the global plastics market include the credit crises in Europe and the United States, as well as China's tight monetary policy, but another key factor is overproduction in the Middle East and China in recent years, resulting in a surplus of 30 million tonnes of plastic goods ... It will take at least five years for this inventory to be consumed."[1]

Central News Agency Taiwan

The fashion industry embedded in consumer society – a model parades at Paris Fashion Week 2014 down a catwalk designed as a supermarket aisle filled with real branded groceries.
Photo: Leandro Justen, BFANYC.com/REX

The disturbing part of all of this is quite how easily it can be pieced together as the consequences of a set of 'rules of the game' and it may be less a set of conscious political decisions than some would imagine: it's a series of outcomes from an iterated system with a history. Inevitably, it carried the seeds of its own limitations: it was always going to do this in the absence of systems level changes. What was a very effective economic machine in a context of cheap and accessible energy and materials has to make way for another operating system, fit for the 21st-century globalised reality. In a few words, we need different rules of the game, if the economy is still to allow us to be 'at home in the modern world'.

Seen in this perspective, the golden generations of those in adulthood in Europe between 1950 and 1979 and in the credit expansion phase 1979-2008 were enjoying a linear economy as good as it (ever) gets.

But what if there was another way of seeing the world, one based in the science of our times, one which entrained systems in a virtuous cycle of capital building rather than in a vicious one where human, social, manufactured and natural capital are transformed into financial capital? All systems have histories and all systems tend to entrain, to draw in and shape relationships and material within their orbit. The linear throughput economy entrains by translating materials into manufactures, or soils into food, via cheap energy, or fisheries into fish fingers. Could we change the rules of the game? Yes we can, and it is in fact fairly intuitive. It is not a new idea, and has been rolling around in different forms for more than 30 years[2] but what is different now is that it has been refined and has begun to engage business in a way that business recognises. More importantly, it is core to understanding where prosperity might come from in a changing world.

It may be the case of 'come the necessity comes the invention', even if people like Walter Stahel have been advocating it since the late 1970s (see Chapter 5). The timing needed to be right. Much has changed which makes this decade the gateway to the circular economy, much of it detailed above and summarised by the phrase 'which way out?' It would be wrong to say that humans have come to their senses, it may be that only now do the advantages seem so clear. Perhaps a little run-through of the basics first.

The old framework was that the world was machine-like. It was deterministic, if you could only find the building blocks and the relationships you could describe the system accurately, or as close enough that it made no difference. In other words, cause and effect writ large: with enough effort it could all be understood. The whole is the sum of the parts. Except that it isn't in most real world systems. The effects of feedback in systems with no fixed initial conditions and many variables has led to an entire area of study called complexity theory.[3] These systems exhibited non-linearity. A certain input might have a disproportionate output and systems at a certain level of complexity might exhibit new, emergent, properties. The coming of the computer allowed humankind to model these dynamic systems, before that the mathematics were complex and laborious to do and the relevance seemed low if the mechanical is assumed to be the general case. One of the first models was Jay Forrester's work, which became the basis of *Limits to Growth* in 1972, with its multiple scenarios around population and resources.

This all might remain something of a 'so-what?' curiosity but for the realisation that as Sally Goerner[4] says: "the vast majority of real-life natural, social and economic phenomena belong to the realm of complexity. Indeed, natural systems, whether physical, social or economic, only rarely exhibit simple causality or weakly connected causality." The conclusion is obvious, the complex iterative system is the general case, often termed 'ordered complexity' (more about this in Chapter 4). It is the name of the game and as Gunter Pauli notes, "thinking in systems and cycles we become metabolists".

It is appropriate to consider the metabolism. Since George Lakoff reminds us that most thought is unconscious and almost all abstract thinking is metaphorical[5] then it seems appropriate for the metabolism to be one of the new core metaphors: it relates to the most elegant of complex systems, life itself. It replaces the machine metaphors, not because it is a trendy choice but because it better reflects the emerging scientific understanding we have about how the universe works. Because it better models how economies work and *that in turn must confer advantages* to practitioners – business.

Ordered, complex, intertwined mutually interdependent systems are the new normal. That is where the economy and business exists, and hence the notion that a circular economy is an expression of systems thinking: an opportunity to upgrade our economics and business to match an expanded, richer vision.

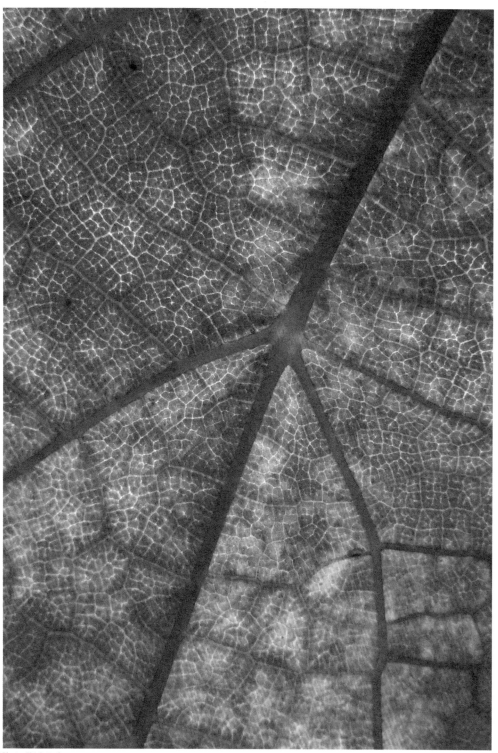

Photo: Thinkstock

Photo: Colin Webster

This chapter comes from 'Towards the circular economy-economic and business rationale for an accelerated transition'. Ellen MacArthur Foundation, 2012.

3 FROM LINEAR TO CIRCULAR

The linear 'make-take-and-dispose' model relies on large quantities of easily accessible resources and energy, and as such is increasingly unfit for the reality in which it operates. Working towards efficiency – a reduction of resources and fossil energy consumed per unit of manufacturing output – will not alter the finite nature of their stocks but can only delay the inevitable. A change of the entire operating system seems necessary.

THE CIRCULAR ECONOMY FRAMEWORK

The circular economy refers to an industrial economy that is restorative by intention; aims to rely on renewable energy; minimises, tracks, and hopefully eliminates the use of toxic chemicals; and eradicates waste through careful design. The term goes beyond the mechanics of production and consumption of goods and services, in the areas that it seeks to redefine (examples include rebuilding capital including social and natural, and the shift from consumer to user). The concept of the circular economy is grounded in the study of non-linear, particularly living systems.

A major outcome of taking insights from living systems is the notion of optimising systems rather than components, which can also be referred to as 'design to fit' – by analogy, the tree is nothing without the forest. It involves a careful management of materials flows, which in the circular economy are of two types as described by McDonough and Braungart (*Cradle to Cradle, Re-making the way we make things*): biological nutrients, designed to re-enter the biosphere safely and build natural capital, and technical nutrients, which are designed to circulate at high quality without entering the biosphere.

As a result, the circular economy draws a sharp distinction between the consumption and use of materials: circular economy advocates the need for a 'functional service' model in which manufacturers or retailers increasingly retain the ownership of their products and, where possible, act as service providers – selling the use of products, not their one-way consumption. This shift has direct implications for the development of efficient and effective take-back systems and the proliferation of product- and business model design practices that generate more durable products, facilitate disassembly and refurbishment and, where appropriate, consider product/service shifts. As circular economy pioneer Walter Stahel explains:

The linear model turned services into products that can be sold, but this throughput approach is a wasteful one. In the past, reuse and service-life extension were often strategies in situations of scarcity or poverty and led to products of inferior quality. Today, they are signs of good resource husbandry and smart management.

Walter Stahel, London, November 2012

DESIGN FOR LIFE

When an item is designed to be a product of service, it is designed to be returned after use, designed for disassembly or repair, designed to be of no harm to user or firm, and to use materials and resources effectively. This is in stark contrast to the usual situation where the design is based on others dealing with end of life, hastening end of life by built-in obsolescence, and using more resources overall (despite increased efficiency in reducing materials used per unit). Design is not for disassembly – since it benefits the recyclers not the manufacturers, and since the product is sold in a price-sensitive market based on throughput there is no incentive to design for durability, rather for low unit cost.

The circular economy tends to internalise costs and in so doing transforms them into benefits – long-lasting, reliable, safe products, easily upgradeable, without end-of-life issues and using materials which do not become waste but which are food for the manufacturer or other firms.

The circular economy is based on a few simple principles:

DESIGN OUT WASTE

Waste does not exist when the biological and technical components (or 'materials') of a product are designed by intention to fit within a biological or technical materials cycle, designed for disassembly and re-purposing. The biological materials are non-toxic and can be simply composted. Technical materials – polymers, alloys and other man-made materials – are designed to be used again with minimal energy and highest quality retention (whereas recycling as commonly understood results in a reduction in quality and feeds back into the process as a crude feedstock). Coined by Braungart and McDonough, the phrase "waste is food" summarises the circular philosophy – though as Braungart himself would say today, "the word waste should not even be in there, there is no such thing, everything should be food."

BUILD RESILIENCE THROUGH DIVERSITY

Modularity, versatility, and adaptivity are prized features that need to be prioritised in an uncertain and fast-evolving world. Diverse systems with many connections and scales are more resilient in the face of external shocks than systems built simply for efficiency – throughput maximisation driven to the extreme results in fragility.

WORK TOWARDS USING ENERGY FROM RENEWABLE SOURCES

Systems should ultimately aim to run on renewable sources. As Vestas, the wind energy company, puts it: "Any circular story should start by looking into the energy involved in the production process". Systems should ultimately aim to run on renewable energy – enabled by the reduced threshold energy levels required by a restorative, circular economy. The agricultural production system solely runs on current solar income but significant amounts of fossil fuels are used in fertilisers, farm machinery, processing and through the supply chain. More integrated food and farming systems would reduce the need for fossil-fuel based inputs and capture more of the energy value of by-products and manures. They would also increase the demand for human labour – which Walter Stahel has argued should be an integral part of this evolution: "Shifting taxation from labour to energy and material consumption would fast-track adoption of more circular business models; it would also make sure that we are putting the efficiency pressure on the true bottleneck of our resource-consuming society/economy – there is no shortage of labour and (renewable) energy in the long term."

THINK IN 'SYSTEMS'

The ability to understand how parts influence one another within a whole, and the relationship of the whole to the parts, is crucial. Elements are considered in relation to their environmental and social contexts. While a machine is also a system, it is clearly narrowly bounded and assumed to be deterministic. Systems thinking usually refers to the overwhelming majority of real-world systems: these are non-linear, feedback-rich, and interdependent. In such systems, imprecise starting conditions combined with feedback lead to often surprising consequences, and to outcomes that are frequently not proportional to the input (runaway or 'undamped' feedback). Such systems cannot be managed in the conventional 'linear' sense, requiring instead more flexibility and more frequent adaptation to changing circumstances.

Systems thinking emphasises stocks and flows. The maintenance or replenishment of stock is inherent in feedback-rich systems, which are assumed to have some longevity, and has the potential to encompass regeneration and even evolution in living systems. In a business context, their modular and adaptive properties mean more leeway for innovation and the development of diversified value chains, as well as less dependence on purely short-term strategies. Understanding flows in complex systems also tells us something more about the trade-off between efficiency and resilience. Systems that are increasingly efficient have fewer nodes, fewer connections, and greater throughput but also become increasingly brittle or, to use Nassim Taleb's term, 'fragile'. This makes them vulnerable to the effects of shocks, like price volatility or interruption of supply. Systems with many nodes and connections are more resilient, but can become sclerotic – slow to change (at the extreme), and thus ineffective.

Effectiveness is the sweet spot where resilience and efficiency interplay: efficiency (doing things right) is welcome, but in the service of effectiveness (doing the right thing), with the prime objective of ensuring the business fits the economy. This is a way of thinking about the idea of systems optimisation. Because more of the flows of materials, goods and services are valorised in a circular economy and because risk is reduced, the firm is compensated for the reduced upside of efficiency with lower costs, additional cash flows and – in many cases – fewer regulatory concerns (as wastes are eliminated, or are now benign flows).

THINK IN CASCADES

For biological materials, the essence of value creation lies in the opportunity to extract additional value from products and materials by cascading them through other applications. In biological decomposition, be it natural or in controlled fermentation processes, material is broken down in stages by microorganisms like bacteria and fungi that extract energy and nutrients from the carbohydrates, fats, and proteins found in the material. For instance, going from tree to furnace forgoes the value that could be harnessed via staged decomposition through successive uses as timber and timber products before decay and eventual incineration.

The complete biological entity should be considered. Mycelium packaging, an innovation based on the bonding properties of mushroom 'roots', uses the entire 'living polymer', as well as the organic waste system on which it grows. A holistic, cascade-based relationship with coffee would consider the entire fruit (the cherry) and the whole coffee-growing protocol. The entire shrub in its context also needs integrating: as a shade-loving plant, it may well be positioned adjacent to other trees. In addition, coffee production generates 12 million tonnes of agricultural waste per year. This waste could be used to replace hardwoods traditionally used as growth media to farm high-value tropical mushrooms, a market with double-digit growth (currently USD 17 billion globally). Coffee waste is in fact a superior medium, as it shortens the production period. The residue (after being used as a growth medium) can be reused as livestock feed, as it contains valuable enzymes, and can be returned to the soil in the form of animal manure.

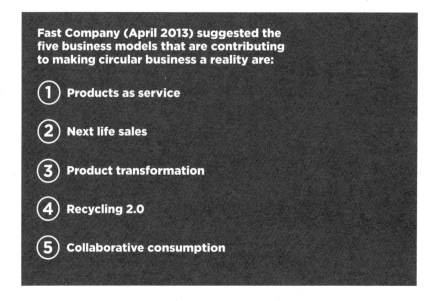

Fast Company (April 2013) suggested the five business models that are contributing to making circular business a reality are:

(1) **Products as service**

(2) **Next life sales**

(3) **Product transformation**

(4) **Recycling 2.0**

(5) **Collaborative consumption**

OVERVIEW OF THE MAIN SCHOOLS OF THOUGHT
The circular economy concept has deep-rooted origins and cannot be traced back to one single date or author. Its practical applications to modern economic systems and industrial processes, however, have gained momentum since the late 1970s led by a small number of academics, thought-leaders and businesses.

The generic concept has been refined and developed
by the following schools of thought:

REGENERATIVE DESIGN
In the US, John T. Lyle started developing ideas on regenerative design that
could be applied to all systems, i.e., beyond agriculture, for which the concept
of regeneration had already been formulated earlier. Arguably, he laid the
foundations of the circular economy framework, which notably developed
and gained prominence thanks to McDonough (who had studied with Lyle),
Braungart and Stahel. Today, the Lyle Center for Regenerative Studies offers
courses on the subject.

PERFORMANCE ECONOMY
Walter Stahel, architect and economist, sketched in his 1976 research report
to the European Commission *The Potential for Substituting Manpower
for Energy*, co-authored with Genevieve Reday, the vision of an economy
in loops (or circular economy) and its impact on job creation, economic
competitiveness, resource savings, and waste prevention. Credited with
having coined the expression 'Cradle to Cradle' in the late 1970s, Stahel
worked at developing a 'closed loop' approach to production processes
and created the Product Life Institute in Geneva more than 25 years
ago. It pursues four main goals: product-life extension, long-life goods,
reconditioning activities, and waste prevention. It also insists on the
importance of selling services rather than products, an idea referred to as
the 'functional service economy', now more widely subsumed into the notion
of 'performance economy'. Stahel argues that the circular economy should
be considered a framework: as a generic notion, the circular economy
draws on several more specific approaches that gravitate around a set of
basic principles.

CRADLE TO CRADLE
German chemist and visionary Michael Braungart went on to develop,
together with American architect Bill McDonough, the Cradle to Cradle™
concept and certification process. This design philosophy considers all
material involved in industrial and commercial processes to be nutrients, of
which there are two main categories: technical and biological. The Cradle to
Cradle framework focuses on design for effectiveness in terms of products
with positive impact and reducing the negative impacts of commerce
through efficiency.

Cradle to Cradle design perceives the safe and productive processes of
nature's 'biological metabolism' as a model for developing a 'technical
metabolism' flow of industrial materials. Product components can be
designed for continuous recovery and reutilisation as biological and
technical nutrients within these metabolisms. The Cradle to Cradle
framework addresses energy and water inputs.

• Eliminate the concept of waste. "Waste equals food." Design products and materials with life cycles that are safe for human health and the environment and that can be reused perpetually through biological and technical metabolisms. Create and participate in systems to collect and recover the value of these materials following their use.
• Power with renewable energy. "Use current solar income." Maximise the use of renewable energy.
• "Celebrate diversity". Manage water use to maximise quality, promote healthy ecosystems and respect local impacts. Guide operations and stakeholder relationships using social responsibility.

INDUSTRIAL ECOLOGY
Industrial ecology is the study of material and energy flows through industrial systems. Focussing on connections between operators within the 'industrial ecosystem', this approach aims at creating closed-loop processes in which waste serves as an input, thus eliminating the notion of an undesirable by-product. Industrial ecology adopts a systemic point of view, designing production processes in accordance with local ecological constraints whilst looking at their global impact from the outset, and attempting to shape them so they perform as close to living systems as possible. This framework is sometimes referred to as the 'science of sustainability', given its interdisciplinary nature, and its principles can also be applied in the services sector. With an emphasis on natural capital restoration, industrial ecology also focuses on social wellbeing.

BIOMIMICRY
Janine Benyus, author of *Biomimicry: Innovation Inspired by Nature,* defines her approach as "a new discipline that studies nature's best ideas and then imitates these designs and processes to solve human problems". Studying a leaf to invent a better solar cell is an example. She thinks of it as 'innovation inspired by nature'. Biomimicry relies on three key principles:

• Nature as model: Study nature's models and emulate these forms, processes, systems, and strategies to solve human problems.
• Nature as measure: Use an ecological standard to judge the sustainability of our innovations.
• Nature as mentor: View and value nature not based on what we can extract from the natural world, but what we can learn from it.

BLUE ECONOMY
Initiated by former Ecover CEO and Belgian businessman Gunter Pauli, the Blue Economy is an open-source movement bringing together concrete case studies, initially compiled in an eponymous report handed over to the Club of Rome. As the official manifesto states, "using the resources available in cascading systems, (...) the waste of one product becomes the input to create a new cash flow". Based on 21 founding principles, the Blue Economy insists on solutions being determined

by their local environment and physical/ecological characteristics, putting the emphasis on gravity as the primary source of energy. The report, which doubles up as the movement's manifesto, describes "100 innovations that can create 100 million jobs within the next 10 years", and provides many examples of winning South-South collaborative projects – another original feature of this approach intent on promoting its hands-on focus.

His focus is most often grass roots entrepreneurship, "substituting something with nothing" and "creating prosperity with what you didn't know you already had". It echoes Amory Lovins when he talks about the main barriers to change being in our heads. Like Lovins and Marcin Jakubowski from the Global Village Construction Set Gunter Pauli believes scarcity is artificial.

The blue economy, akin to Jakubowski's 'open source economy', is a serious initiative around rethinking the economy from the basics and encouraging entrepreneurship at the grassroots. In passing, Gunter uses the term blue economy as a way of challenging advocates of a command economy (red) and a green economy (only for the well-off consumer). As 'blue' is the colour of the planet seen from space, it is meant to convey a big picture significance.

PERMACULTURE
Australian ecologists Bill Mollison and David Holmgren coined the term 'permaculture' in the late 1970s, defining it as "the conscious design and maintenance of agriculturally productive ecosystems, which have the diversity, stability and resilience of natural ecosystems". Considerable interest in the concept exists around the globe, propelled by thinkers and practitioners like Masanobu Fukuoka in Japan and Sepp Holzer in Austria. Permaculture draws elements from both traditional sustainable agriculture and modern innovations and principles. Permaculture systems improve yields and diets while reducing water consumption, improving soil quality and restoring biodiversity. Permaculture integrates elements from agroforestry (forest farming, alley cropping, windbreaks), conservation agriculture (fertiliser trees, no till and uncompacted soils, permanent soil cover), organic agriculture (organic inputs and on-site nutrient recycling), and traditional agriculture (rainwater harvesting and water infiltration, including key-line design and tied contour bunds). Further aspects it covers are sustainable livestock management (integrated crop-livestock systems) for subsistence smallholders and commercial operations, and agro-ecology (the optimal selection of system elements originating in different times and places). It deploys methods that are compatible with the sustained intensification of production. In the public perception it is associated with local and/or small scale operations which require extensive knowledge and application to succeed.

This table contrasts linear and circular modes for the general elucidation of the idea that systems entrain and the consequences are much less a matter of choice at an individual level than might be supposed. If extending and exploiting circularity in business is

Linear	Circular	Notes
Externalises costs in search of production cost reduction	Internalises costs in search for quality service/ performance and low risk	*Refers to manufactures like white goods of medium complexity, especially those with reasonable use periods*
POS = point of sale and ends most responsibility	Usually rent/lease/recovery but business extends responsibility. POS = point of service	*If biological pathway assumes non-toxic "waste = food" consumption via appropriate cascading*
Creates waste streams for municipalities and individuals to deal with	Reduces waste streams and provides value streams instead	*Might reduce GDP as this does not distinguish between 'goods' and 'bads' in its calculation*
Promotes global scale in production to secure low costs and market position	Regional and local scales feasible as value is more in the service provided than the selling of product	*Note changing approaches to manufactures – e.g. devolved digital manufacturing*
Encourages standardisation to add to efficiency/ease of consumption	Encourages standardisation of components and protocols to encourage repair, recovery and reuse	*Open source – download designs not ship products*
Consumption turnover encouraged – planned obsolescence etc. Possession trumps access	User mentality, trouble free service or performance sought (reliability). Less turnover. Access trumps possession	*Huge opportunity for marketeers to profit from this*
Economic growth driven by compound interest and money as debt	Investing in restorative long-term schemes driven by complementary currencies	*Reverses the effect of net present value calculations*
Prices reflect only the private costs of production distribution, sale etc.	Prices reflect the full costs aided by reduction of externalised costs	

one key aim, we need to know how a subtle change of the rules of the game might have far-reaching consequences over time. There is nothing here about explicit social policy or political systems. A circular economy can work under a whole range of arrangements.

Linear	Circular	Notes
Tax on labour encourages labour productivity (substitute capital or energy). Reduces employment if growth not strong	Taxes off income and other renewables and on waste, non-renewables, unearned income. Increases employment generally as a result of reduced cost of labour	
Recycling represents another raw material flow and ignores lost embodied energy and quality	Recycling represents a low grade option – an outer loop. Sometimes necessary	*Recycling legitimises a linear economy by promising what it cannot possibly achieve – a closed loop on short-cycle, low-value materials*
Transforms natural and social capital into financial capital via a short-term preference – rapid, large flows	(Re)builds capital (stocks) from which to derive more and better flows over the longer term	*Assumes in circular economy that natural and social capital are degraded at starting point*
As the throughput model externalises costs there is a truncated materials flow to concern the product designers	As the product and service are wholly dependent on a functioning materials flow which is 'closed loop' the 'fit' is imperative. Whole systems design indicated	
Economic growth evolves to become a need to offset labour productivity and to meet interest payments	Economic growth replaced by more sophisticated measure: assumes increasing prosperity and well being as part of a restorative cycle	*A long-standing discussion*
Production> sale in a linear system can be very competitive for product sales and market share in the context of need for low costs and thus economies of scale, often global (supply push for branded products)	Whole systems design is inherently more 'we' than 'me' orientated. Cooperation will be required as well as competition. Markets, regional or local, perhaps more differentiated (demand pull for generic products)	
Basic metaphor is 'world as machine and parts'. Humans can understand predict and control. Individual is centre of the world and can work instrumentally to achieve ever greater results	Basic metaphor is of living systems -'metabolisms' – where we have complex relationships in which we are participants, have influence and limited opportunity to understand (we need to review frequently)	*The general case is one where the system is non-linear, the special or less common case is the linear*

Table ©Ellen MacArthur Foundation/Ken Webster 2013

Photo: Jocelyn Blériot

4 THROUGH THE MACROSCOPE

> **The key to complexity is systems thinking. The key to systems thinking is Patterns; and, the key to using Patterns is to form them into a language.**
> Christopher Alexander

Until the beginning of the 20th century, scientific method was developed around the worldview that everything was mechanical in character, it was 'machine-like'.

This 'world as machine' was a fine idea and was used to search for the building blocks and then the mechanisms in every one of the emerging disciplines: in physics, chemistry, medicine, engineering, biology (where Darwin had such an influence at a later date). It had application and was just a better way of getting things done: it had consequences and the industrial revolution was just one. The idea applied as much in the social realm through the new studies of psychology, sociology and of course in that branch of natural philosophy called economics, all of which soon wanted to be quantitative sciences. In economics the market became the mechanism for deciding resource allocation, and the individual as consumer and as business (producer) or worker was best served by a free exchange, open information, many buyers and sellers and the rational, welfare-maximising 'homo economicus'. Anything less would restrict the market mechanism.

More broadly, the individual as the 'atom of society' was not only able to make her own approach to the Divine, rather than through the priest, by being able to read the Bible in her own language, but she was also to begin shaking off irrational arrangements in all else, from social duties to business, to denounce them, as in the example above, a hindrance on trade – the rationale of trade being the market. It became commonplace to point to the individual, or the individual business (when they became legal entities as corporations) as the rational focus for all economic choices and benefits deployed through the market. Welcome to the modern world. And it worked. For a time it was almost deified as 'Progress' with a capital 'P'.

The modern world became the expression of an idea or framework, and in common with all abstract ideas – these grand metanarratives – it used a self-referencing set of metaphors to express its meaning. This is the 'world as machine' metaphor, unsurprisingly. Thus, so often is largeness and scale celebrated, because this is meant to be efficiency deployed in a grand manner. It was an era of mass production and mass consumption.

And in resource and energy terms the economy was a machine for turning materials and energy into producer and consumer goods and services. Since resources and resourcefulness were as endless as the oil gushing from the wells of West Texas and Persia, more and faster and more efficiently were the keys to surplus which in turn made everyone richer. A machine world, manufacturing prosperity endlessly ...

In general, Enlightenment 1.0, as sketched above, is quite a long story and a successful one. It enabled artillery shells and moonshots, the Model T Ford, the elimination of many diseases, the creation of atomic bombs, and the feeding of some billion more people who could not subsist otherwise. It's all around us.

However it is not the full story, it is not a case of carry on regardless. This mechanistic worldview, and thus the economy built on it, is inadequate, or incomplete.

Joël de Rosnay takes up the story.[1]... He suggests that the classical thought detailed above has an over-emphasis on analysis and that this should be balanced by synthesis, and more.

> **To the opposition of analytic and systemic we must add the opposition of static vision and dynamic vision. Our knowledge of nature and the major scientific laws rests on what I shall call 'classic thought', which has three main characteristics. Its concepts have been shaped in the image of a 'solid' (conservation of form, preservation of volume, effects of force, spatial relations, hardness, solidity).**
>
> **Irreversible time, that of life's duration, of the non-determined, of chance events is never taken into account. All that counts is physical time and reversible phenomena. T can be changed to -T without modifying the phenomena under study.**
>
> **The only form of explanation of phenomena is linear causality; that is, the method of explanation relies on a logical sequence of cause and effect that extends for its full dimension along the arrow of time.**

Are you ready to be discomforted?

About forty-five years ago a number of Massachusetts Institute of Technology staff and alumni, including Joël de Rosnay (a Mauritian-born French science writer, futurist and molecular biologist), began to compare our usual means of seeing: the microscope, for detail, the infinitely small, and the telescope for distance, the infinitely great, with what the emerging science around systems was demanding – a macroscope. A device that dropped the detail and revealed the big picture, the overview, the infinitely complex, the pattern.

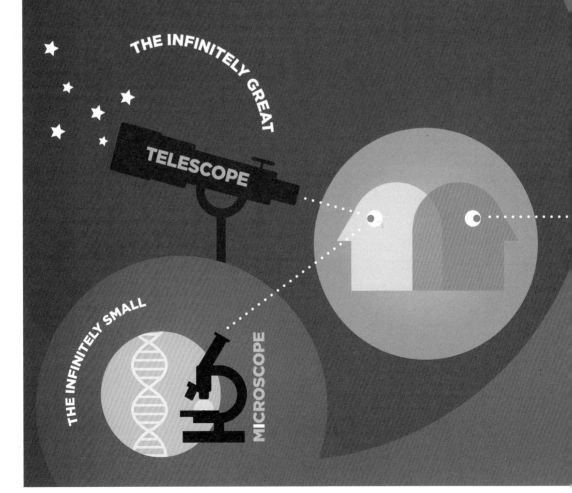

THE INFINITELY GREAT

TELESCOPE

THE INFINITELY SMALL

MICROSCOPE

> To raise new questions, new possibilities, to regard old problems from a new angle, requires creative imagination and marks real advance in science.
> **Albert Einstein**

THE INFINITELY COMPLEX

NATURE SOCIETY

MACROSCOPE

Joël de Rosnay, *The Macroscope* (1979)

In present modes of thought, influenced by the systemic approach, the concept of the fluid replaces that of the solid. Movement replaces permanence. Flexibility and adaptability replace rigidity and stability.

The concepts of flow and flow equilibrium are added to those of force and force equilibrium. Duration and irreversibility enter as basic dimensions in the nature of phenomena. Causality becomes circular and opens up to finality. The dynamics of systems shatters the static vision of organisations and structures; by integrating time it makes manifest *relatedness* and *development*. Another table may help to enlighten and enrich the most important concepts related to classic thought and systemic thought.

The following table compares, one by one, the traits of the two approaches:

ANALYTIC APPROACH

ISOLATES then concentrates on the elements

STUDIES the nature of interaction

EMPHASISES the precision of details

MODIFIES one variable at a time

REMAINS independent of duration of time; the phenomena considered are reversible

VALIDATES facts by means of experimental proof within the body of a theory

USES PRECISE AND DETAILED MODELS that are less useful in actual operation (example: econometric models)

HAS AN EFFICIENT APPROACH when interactions are linear and weak

LEADS TO DISCIPLINE-ORIENTED (juxtadisciplinary) education

LEADS TO ACTION programmed in detail

POSSESSES KNOWLEDGE of details; poorly defined goals

SYSTEMIC APPROACH

UNIFIES and concentrates on the interaction between elements

STUDIES the effects of interactions

EMPHASISES global perception

MODIFIES groups of variables simultaneously

INTEGRATES duration of time and irreversibility

VALIDATES facts through comparison of the behaviour of the model with reality

USES MODELS that are insufficiently rigorous to be used as bases of knowledge but are useful in decision and action (example: models of the Club of Rome)

HAS AN EFFICIENT APPROACH when interactions are non-linear and strong

LEADS TO MULTIDISCIPLINARY education

LEADS TO ACTION through objectives

POSSESSES KNOWLEDGE of goals, fuzzy detail

Hence the need for the macroscope and, with it, the understanding of dynamic systems, systems with feedback but uncertainty.[2] Hence too the need for the skills of seeing the big picture, of being empathetic, seeing from another's point of view, since one of the lessons of feedback and interdependence is that of unforeseen or unexpected outcomes in both near but also distant parts of the system.

Nor is this rebalancing of the activities of the mind just a special pleading. Far from it. The diagram below illustrates the distribution of different types of system and how we might deal with it. It shows the mechanical (linear) and statistical (disordered complexity) as very much in the tails of the distribution of systems overall. The conclusion is obvious, the complex iterative system is the general case, often termed 'ordered complexity'.

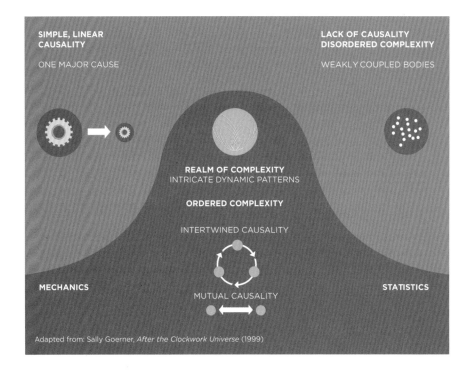

SIMPLE, LINEAR
CAUSALITY

ONE MAJOR CAUSE

LACK OF CAUSALITY
DISORDERED COMPLEXITY

WEAKLY COUPLED BODIES

REALM OF COMPLEXITY
INTRICATE DYNAMIC PATTERNS

ORDERED COMPLEXITY

INTERTWINED CAUSALITY

MECHANICS

MUTUAL CAUSALITY

STATISTICS

Adapted from: Sally Goerner, *After the Clockwork Universe* (1999)

The shock for some, for many actually, is the flipping of what appears to matter most. Many people, adults as well as the young, still believe that the world is basically ordered in a way which makes the 'linear' model dominant, the common sense *general case*, and that there are exceptions and, yes, uncertainties. But people believe these can be taken 'on advisement', something to be conscious of but little more, the *special case*. Where there is order it is approximately mechanical, and statistics can be used if the disordered must be looked at.

The graphic (see previous page) shows that the mechanical and the completely disordered are in fact quite unusual, limited cases of real world systems, and even the graphic does too much to honour the tails (it's illustrative only). Almost all real world systems are *ordered complexity:* they are the bound-up, feedback-rich, deeply interdependent systems that systems thinking tries to assist with.

This is an enormous challenge. In the real world an economics which has aspirations to be a science will be based around the notions of non-linear systems, will be embedded in flows of materials, energy and information (not just income and capital flows), will be managed not by crude levers or assumed to work perfectly – if only it were left uncluttered.

The economy, like all non-linear examples of ordered complexity, can be influenced, and because iterations, those feedback loops, have such a powerful effect it is more a matter of 'setting the rules of the game' and watching carefully the many consequences, then adjusting variables, not one at a time but simultaneously. And, of course, due attention to the 'systemic' column of the table (see page 69) makes a lot of sense in management science too, though its application there is limited at present.

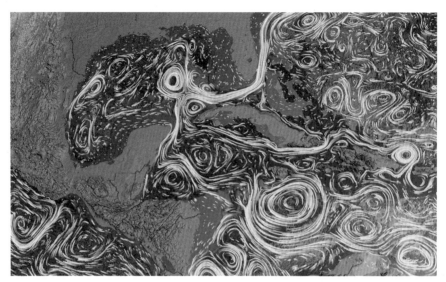

Visualization shows ocean surface currents around the Gulf of Mexico and the
Caribbean Sea during the period from June 2005 through December 2007.
Source: NASA Goddard Centre.

Elsewhere in the book is a debate about efficiency (See Chapter 5):
surely, more efficiency is good when it comes to using fewer materials
or less energy, but a single focus on efficiency rather than on
optimising the whole can have consequences which are self-defeating,
e.g. if overall demand goes up or spending is liberated for other areas –
the story of silver and its use in photography is a case in point.

Digital photography has taken over from photography based on film
in the past 10 years. The film was made using silver compounds and
the demand for silver for this purpose was 25% of the total demand at
its peak in 2000. It is now around 9% and falling. This could be seen
as a way of the photography industry getting materials efficiency by
substituting digits for silver. So what happened to silver production and
prices? The graph opposite is instructive. Silver prices and production
went up despite this, much of it becoming coins and 'investment'–
hoarding bullion bars.

DIGITAL PHOTOGRAPHY AND SILVER PRODUCTION

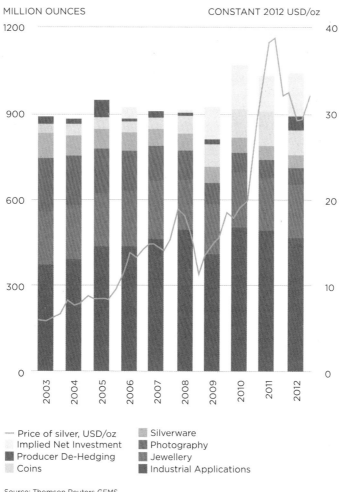

MILLION OUNCES   CONSTANT 2012 USD/oz

Legend:
- — Price of silver, USD/oz
- Implied Net Investment
- Producer De-Hedging
- Coins
- Silverware
- Photography
- Jewellery
- Industrial Applications

Source: Thomson Reuters GFMS

There are examples
in nature that exhibit
fractal-like properties,
such as ferns.

Photo: Thinkstock

A circular economy is surely to be discussed in a way which acknowledges the notion of complex interactions, iteration (feedback) and uncertainty, and not discussed, say, on the basis of 'recovering useful material from waste streams' or 'recycling' because it assumes these can be pretty self-contained, i.e. it slips back into too narrow a conceptualisation.

Design is key to a circular economy, we are told. According to Nigel Cross, a leader in design thinking:

> **Scientific problem solving is done by analysis, while designers problem solve through synthesis.**

This fits very well with a systems perspective.

If it's a feedback-rich systems perspective it's about the whole cycle and a key question is whether interventions are enriching or depleting the overall system. A positive regenerative cycle is sought, without doubt.

A little more about systems thinking basics. In short, it's about iteration, which means feedback loops and their effect. There are two types of feedback, *reinforcing* (sometimes called positive feedback) and *balancing* (sometimes called negative feedback), coupled to uncertain starting positions and many *interrelated* cycles at *different scales.* Fractals are the result of iterating with positive and negative feedback at many scales with built-in uncertainty.

The result of iterations can be a durable system; it has coherence and continuity but in a wholly dynamic way. A machine might come to rest but a dynamic system can boom, bust or achieve a dynamic balance. It is never at rest. It need not be complicated: imagine a person standing on a plank over a log, constantly adjusting to maintain their balance.

De Rosnay summarises:

"A complex system is made up of a large *variety* of components or elements that possess specialised functions. These elements are organised in internal hierarchical *levels* (in the human body, for example, cells, organs, and systems of organs). The different levels and individual elements are linked by a great variety of *bonds*. Consequently there is a high concentration of interconnections. The interactions between the elements of a complex system are of a particular type; they are *nonlinear* interactions."

De Rosnay provided a number of diagrams in his book *The Macroscope* to illustrate different types of feedback:

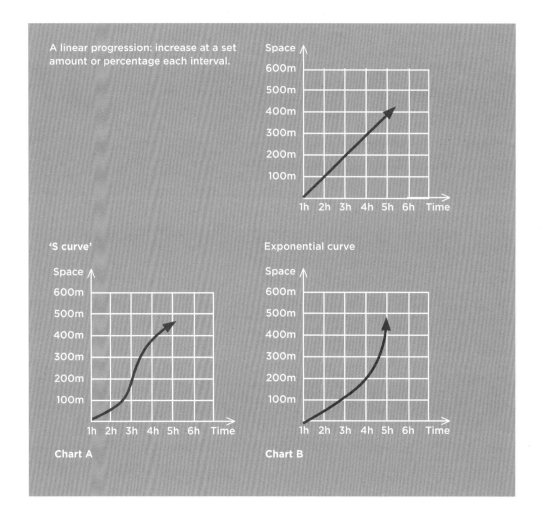

A linear progression: increase at a set amount or percentage each interval.

'S curve'

Chart A

Exponential curve

Chart B

The exponential curve (chart B), shows feedback in the form familiar in compound interest, where the interest is rolled into the amount after each interval and interest applied to the whole. Chart A, balancing feedback or changing conditions – approaching limits – constrain or reduce the rate of increase, e.g. world population in recent years is increasing at a decreasing rate.

The feedback graph below right shows this exponential reinforcing feedback. Every iteration reinforces the trajectory, either towards explosion (boom!) or collapse (bust). Think of bacteria in a petri dish, booming until there is no more easy food and then eventually collapsing as food runs out.

To the left is the balancing or negative feedback. The starting position is varied, either above or below a desired equilibrium, and the feedback moves it towards the equilibrium – the thermostat might record that the room temperature is below the set level and turn on the furnace. But only when the equilibrium is reached does the thermostat shut off the furnace and there is a lag in the system with some heat coming through, so the measure overshoots, and the process works in reverse; in turn, this overshoots and then recovers. A tendency towards the equilibrium is the result. But neither of these simplifications is enough since starting conditions are not fixed in real systems, and the interplay between positive and negative feedbacks is complex. This uncertainty creates a topography, the pattern of a system's activity over time (see the Lorenz attractor drawing overleaf).

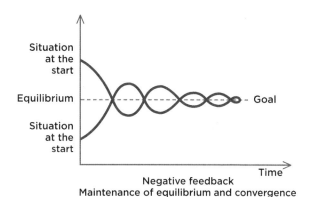

Negative feedback
Maintenance of equilibrium and convergence

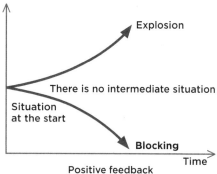

Positive feedback
Exponential growth and divergent behaviour

A topography - the Lorenz attractor

Photos: Thinkstock

"It appears to be a general principle that pulsing systems prevail in the long run, perhaps because they generate more productivity, power, and performance than steady states or those that boom and bust... Operations that pulse transform more energy than those at steady state."

In observing living systems Odum and Odum[3] in the above quote talk about the cycle of growth, maturity, decay and reordering as very dynamic, as a pulse, and that this is indeed a very effective arrangement.

De Rosnay wrote before the major developments around visualising ordered complexity which have followed the work of meteorologist Edward Lorenz and mathematician Benoit Mandlebrot, and the initial enthusiasm around 'chaos theory', but after the use of early computer modelling, which had produced the seminal Club of Rome report *The Limits to Growth*. This publication set off the debate around global resources, the effects of which are still playing out today. Complex global systems require modelling to draw out significance and the results of systems iterating over time are patterns; they do not constitute a result since none exists in the naïve sense, but over time topographies or landscapes of states of the system do develop. It is interesting to think that more powerful computing allowed us to see the dynamic world in a way we had not fully explored hitherto, yet it had been staring us in the face all of the time. But even so... the classical thought still seems to

dominate. The weather forecast is still complained about because it is not accurate, yet it is helpful; it is giving a context and some possibilities. That is what's possible. The government is supposed to be in control of the economy so gets the blame when it doesn't work out. But the economy is not a machine and the effects of leverage are barely understood. The government might influence but is not in control. The events of 2007/8 in the financial markets were not supposed to happen because the risks had been covered – a failure to understand that iterated systems will always experience unusual events, disproportionate events: propping up a bank's insurance cover for USD 300 million of risk is nothing if the liability looks like USD 300 billion.

The famous butterfly effect, where a butterfly's wing disturbs an airflow in Bishkek and this disturbance is for once iterated through a system so that eventually it becomes a tornado in Japan, has been portrayed in recent advertising as a series of escalating consequences, of mishaps in a neighbourhood which include squirrels, cars and boats. The latter is a linear sequence of events and nothing to do with a butterfly effect, which is within one system, the weather system. Regardless of the advertiser's understanding or intention, this portrayal points to and perpetuates a deep popular misunderstanding.[4]

Here is a useful summary diagram around different modes of thought. It is important to remember that it is not an 'either/or', just a call for including them all, and understanding their value.

STATIC VISION
(SIMPLE SYSTEMS)

DYNAMIC VISION
(COMPLEX SYSTEMS)

 SOLID

 FLUID

 FORCE

 FLOW

 CLOSED SYSTEM

 OPEN SYSTEM

 LINEAR CAUSALITY
- STABILITY
- RIGIDITY
- SOLIDITY

 CIRCULAR CAUSALITY
- DYNAMIC STABILITY
- STATIONARY STATE
- CONTINUOUS TURNOVER

 FORCE EQUILIBRIUM

 FLOW EQUILIBRIUM

 EXAMPLE: A CRYSTAL

 EXAMPLE: A CELL

BEHAVIOUR OF SYSTEMS
- FORSEEABLE
- REPRODUCIBLE
- REVERSIBLE

BEHAVIOUR OF SYSTEMS
- UNFORSEEABLE
- UNREPRODUCIBLE
- IRREVERSIBLE

Adapted from Joël de Rosnay, *The Macroscope* (1979)

And what value does it have for a revised economy, for a business, say?

The analytical, the reductionist, and 'can do' attitude often assumes the ends are given.

The role of the firm is to maximise return for its shareholders or, to be more realistic, to maximise the opportunities for remuneration for its controlling managers. This relates to things like market share or sales as much as profit. But, as this book seeks to show, the 'smash and grab' and 'be the biggest', which work so well in a planet with effectively endless resources of material and energy, and huge opportunities for labour productivity, simply do not work when the easy surplus has gone. Prosperity requires a different emphasis: more co-operation, more symbiosis perhaps. A systems approach can help, as the requisites in such uncertain, game-changing times are innovation and creativity. In fact, a systems understanding reminds us that survival of the fittest means the firm *which fits best into its context* – and context is inescapable. The strongest trees are in the healthiest forest.

❝ The systemic approach catalyses imagination, creativity, and invention. It is the foundation of inventive thought (where the analytical approach is the foundation of knowledgeable thought). Tolerant and pragmatic, systemic thought is open to analogy, metaphor, and model – all formerly excluded from 'the scientific method' and now rehabilitated. Everything that unlocks knowledge and frees imagination is welcomed by the systemic approach; it will remain open, like the systems it studies. ❞
Joël de Rosnay

The use of the macroscope and the application of systems approaches, not least the interplay between efficiency and resilience, between the risks of brittleness (too much efficiency) and stagnation (too little, or too slow a flow) are becoming tools in themselves.

Speaking in 2009, Andy Haldane, the executive director for financial stability at the Bank of England, remarked: "Seizures in the electricity grid, degradation of ecosystems, the spread of epidemics and the disintegration of the financial system – each is essentially a different branch of the same network family tree... Theoretical developments in statistical physics and complex systems may be able to help."[5]

There is a long way to go before the impacts of systems insights are fully developed and the implications for education and training in this context are huge. Progress is slow however. Over twenty years ago, educationalist Bela Benathy wrote:

"Much of the learning we offer today is still grounded in the perceptions and practices of the bygone industrial age. In order to free education from the bondage of the past a major shift has to take place, not only in the way we perceive the role and function of education but also in the learning experiences we should offer"[6]

It is freeing education from the bondage of the past and it is, by stages, surely freeing business and industry, or even government from the bygone age too, the one dominated by the linear economy and a one-sided reductionist, linear mindset. The two are profoundly interlinked and it will be fruitless to expect business to lead on the basis of new opportunities and new business models if the vitality of its young intakes – from what is an ever more expensive and extended education process – is still restricted by the residual prejudices and practices of Enlightenment 1.0.

It is for reasons like this that such an emphasis is laid on the shift from a linear economy being part of a more general rethinking, be it prompted by materials and energy, price volatility and supply issues or not, and it is something which has been in process since the early cybernetics

> **A pattern is essentially a morphological law, a relationship among parts within a particular context. Specifically, a pattern expresses a relationship among parts that resolves problems that would exist if the relationship were missing. As patterns express these relationships, they are not formulae or algorithms, but rather loose rules of thumb or heuristics.[7]**

and systems approaches in MIT after World War 2. The rehabilitation of the systemic alongside the analytic is nothing less than an imperative, a consequence of having a civilisation built, so we are told, on science and reason and made valid – lest we forget that some forms of political activity are more feedback-driven than others – by active citizenship in a democracy. Systems thinking indicates that all participation matters.

To return to the first two of the short statements about systems: the key to understanding complexity is systems thinking (see Christopher Alexander quote page 64). And the key to systems thinking is Pattern. Almost all real world systems are ordered complexity and the results of ordered complexity are visible everywhere in patterns, self-similarity at every level, nested systems, fractals and these in turn have strong mathematical roots, and modelling is essential to the unfoldment of meaning: the search for stable and unstable patterns, and the search for the periodicity of key events and cycles is important.

The third key to understanding patterns, according to Christopher Alexander, is in developing a language and this is often perceived as the hardest part. It is true in music and economics and business as much as physics or maths. Unfamiliar terms abound but visually it is becoming easier to recognise: uncertain starting conditions, iteration, an interplay between reinforcing and balancing feedback loops, bifurcation points and normal and strange attractors, topographies and entailment, emergent behaviour, the adaptive cycle. Equally the human is a pattern-seeking animal who can make judgements and 'read' buildings, spaces, streets and their relationship to one another intuitively and sense what 'feels right'. It is perhaps no surprise that one of the greatest exponents of the role of this skill, of making explicit pattern language, is an architect, Christopher Alexander, whose works *A Timeless Way of Building* and *A Pattern Language* have found a resonance and value with object-orientated computer programmers, educators and online community developers.

Photo: Thinkstock

"Integrity is the essence of everything successful."

Buckminster Fuller

SHIFT TO RENEWABLES

El Hierro is the most western of the seven Canary islands – with a population of just over 10,500 – and declared a UNESCO biosphere reserve in the year 2000. From the air it looks mostly barren – partially moonlike, partially overgrown with shrubs and a few scattered palm trees on the coast. The volcanic history of the island is evident: the island rises from sea level to up to 1,500 metres of elevation in just a few kilometres.

In 2002, the Cabildo (local government) approved an ambitious project: turning the island self-sustainable with renewable energy.

The idea is very systemic: five Enercon wind turbines of 2.3 MWp each will generate up to 11.5 MW of electrical power for the island's consumption. With current peak demand at 7 MW, up to one third of the energy can be stored when the turbines are operated at full power. This takes place in the form of water pumped into a deposit of half a million cubic metres. From there, the water is released into two aerial pipelines when wind power is too low – over a length of 3km (530m underground), a difference of nearly 700 metres in altitude leads to up to 11.3 MWp of hydro power to substitute times of less wind. The ingenuity of the project lies in the details: the majority of the electrical energy used on El Hierro is required to run the three desalination plants to generate drinking water. Around 70–80% of this water is used for agriculture. So what at first seems like a simple energy project is in fact a project to provide self-sufficiency to an island that always suffered from scarcity of water and thus food. In the medium term, El Hierro has planned to install a second storage system for its excess energy: electric cars with exchangeable batteries will replace 40% of the vehicles on the island (around 4,500 vehicles) by 2020. The energy alone will save USD 1.8 million per annum currently spent on 6,000 tonnes of diesel which will be substituted, as well as saving emissions of 18,700 tonnes of CO_2. However, when e-mobility comes into play, significant additional savings become possible – and all that money will circulate in and strengthen the local economy, no longer leaving the island. The local government also has the vision to be able to provide the water generated from the island's own energy cheaper to the farmers – in return for farmers agreeing to switch to organic agriculture (the fusion of energy and water utilities has not yet been achieved). Several other sources of renewable energy could be tapped in future, such as solar-thermal and photovoltaic – the Canary Islands know only an average of 35 days of rain every year, the rest is mostly pure sunshine!

El Hierro is a small island, but it's instructive ... considering that 17 million Europeans and 600 million people worldwide live on islands, many of them remote.

Source: *A Blue Economy. A Report About El Hierro* (May 2012)

Photo: Image Broker/Rex

Written by Walter R Stahel

A fully referenced version of this chapter can be found in *A New Dynamic: Effective Business in a Circular Economy* (Ellen MacArthur Foundation, 2013). It is reprinted in this slightly amended form with the kind permission of Walter Stahel.

Photo: Jocelyn Blériot

5 CONSUMER TO USER

> The business angle of a circular economy – higher competitiveness, higher resource security and material efficiency.
>
> Walter R Stahel

"**Previous patterns of growth have brought increased prosperity, but through intensive and often inefficient use of resources. The role of biodiversity, ecosystems and their services is largely undervalued, the costs of waste are often not reflected in prices, current markets and public policies cannot fully deal with competing demands on strategic resources such as minerals, land, water and biomass. This calls for a coherent and integrated response over a wide range of policies in order to deal with expected resource constraints and to sustain our prosperity in the long run.**"

This statement by the European Commission (2011) analyses today's resource efficiency and policy shortcomings. But it does not give solutions, it does not address labour as a resource and it leaves out a number of other challenges.

Economic actors in the circular economy have started to tackle many of these issues in a bottom-up approach by introducing new private sector business models of the circular economy, such as 'reuse, repair and remanufacture instead of replace', and 'selling goods as services'.

This includes an efficient use of labour as a renewable resource with a qualitative edge and "an economy as if people mattered" (E F Schumacher).

The multiple advantages of a circular economy were described decades ago by Stahel and Reday, and have started to transcend into policy making, as for instance in the 2008 EU waste directive. However, politicians' reflexes are still geared to overcome economic problems by promoting growth in the industrial production economy – witness the 'cash for clunkers' initiatives in 22 countries in 2010 – or by focussing on singular issues, such as environmental solutions. The quest for sustainable (holistic) solutions, which would simultaneously address economic, social and environmental issues, is jeopardised by the 'silo' structures of public administrations, academia and many corporations. Stahel showed that most sustainable solutions are intersectoral and interdisciplinary and thus contradict existing regulations, do not fit into academic career structures and demand a 'new think'.

This chapter shows the advantages inherent in the circular economy and argues that the shift to a circular economy can be accelerated by one simple shift in public policy – adapting the tax system to the principles of sustainability by not taxing renewable resources, including work. This will bring about a rapid expansion not only of the circular economy for manufactured capital (infrastructure, equipment and goods) but equally of all other economic activities based on stock optimisation and 'caring', such as health services, education, organic agriculture, producing goods from such locally available renewable materials as leather, wood and wool. Caring is also the foundation for maintaining our cultural heritage.

"The goods of today are the resources of tomorrow at yesterday's prices.

Walter R Stahel **"**

A CIRCULAR ECONOMY IS ABOUT
ECONOMICS AND PROFIT MAXIMISATION

This section details the circular economy, its focus on stock optimisation, and its structure of three loops of different nature and five principles. It explains why reuse and service-life extension of goods are the most profitable and resource efficient business models of the circular economy. From an economics view, maintaining value and performance of stock replaces value added of flow, and utilisation value replaces exchange value as central notion of economic value.

Before 2012, few studies existed which analysed the economic benefits of a circular economy on a national or supranational level. In time for the World Economic Forum 2012 in Davos, the UK-based Ellen MacArthur Foundation published a report which calculates that a circular economy (better design and more efficient use of material) could save European manufacturers USD630 billion a year by 2025. The report, produced by consultancy McKinsey, only covers five sectors that represent a little less than half of the GDP contribution of EU manufacturing, but still calculates that greater resource efficiency could deliver multi-billion Euro savings equivalent to 23 percent of current spending on manufacturing inputs.

The following abstract of *The Product-Life Factor* for the Mitchell Prize Competition 1982 on 'The role of the private sector in a sustainable society' is still an excellent summary of the circular economy:

"The extension of the use-life of goods is, first, a sensible point at which to start a gradual transition towards a sustainable society in which progress is made consistent with the world's finite resource base and, second, a strategy consistent with an active and independent role for the private sector. Product-life, or the period over which products and goods are used, governs their replacement speed and thus the consumption of natural resources required for their manufacture and the amount of waste they create. Shortening product-life increases demand for replacement goods where these can be afforded. Extending product-life optimises the total life-span of goods and reduces depletion of natural resources and consequently waste; it builds on and increases wealth. Compared to fast-replacement, product-life extension is a substitution of service activities for extractive and manufacturing Industries, and a replacement of large-scale capital-intensive companies by smaller, labour-intensive, locally integrated work units. The private sector, whether R&D, manufacturing or finance, will find innumerable business opportunities in product-life extension activities – reuse, repair, reconditioning and recycling.

Indeed, while increasing the number of skilled jobs available and reducing our dependence on strategic materials, such activities will provide the private sector with fresh impetus to make cheaper goods available as part of a self-replenishing economy built on a closed-loop pattern which allows a substitution of manpower for energy. In this way, unemployment and poverty which certainly aggravate the fundamental instability of the world economy might be substantially reduced. The private sector has, moreover, resources and skills that uniquely qualify it to initiate this transition towards a sustainable society where a balanced use of resources and other societal goals are achieved. Potential disincentives and obstacles can, we believe, be overcome with appropriate education and fiscal and policy measures."

A circular economy is about stock optimisation. New metrics to measure changes in the quantity and quality of stock – wealth in the form of manufactured capital stock, but also of health, education and skills – are needed to manage stock. We know how much money governments spend on building schools and employing teachers, but we do not know if as a result the students are better prepared for life. The stock of buildings in a given country and their qualitative conditions (thermal insulation, annual energy consumption) are not known, nor the residual service-life of infrastructure or technical equipment – which makes a national stock and thus wealth management difficult.

Turning the linear industrial economy into a loop or circular economy is, by definition, reducing the economic importance of resource extraction and waste management, and also reducing the environmental impairment caused by these industrial sectors. This change of focus from a linear throughput to a stock management opens opportunities in three loops of different characteristics, which are described in this

section and shown graphically in the figure on page 96:
(a) a reuse and remarketing loop for goods,
(b) a loop of product-life extension activities of goods, and
(c) a recycling loop for molecules (secondary resources).

Buying performance - Rolls Royce engine and 'power by the hour'
Photo: Rolls Royce

A circular economy is characterised by a number of principles which do not exist in the linear industrial economy, with the exception of principle 5. Policy makers and economic actors of the manufacturing economy therefore do not recognise them, nor their impact on the economy:

The smaller the loop (activity-wise and geographically) the more profitable and resource efficient it is.

Loops have no beginning and no end.

The speed of the circular flows is crucial: the efficiency of managing stock in the circular economy increases with a decreasing flow speed.

Continued ownership is cost efficient: reuse, repair and remanufacture without a change of ownership saves double transaction costs.

A circular economy needs functioning markets.

THE MAIN LOOPS OF A CIRCULAR ECONOMY

MANUFACTURING

1

UTILISATION > WASTE

RESOURCES > BASE MATERIALS

REUSE & REMARKETING

2

1 **Junction 1 product-life extension v new goods**
Cost advantage product-life extension

Loop 1 re-use of goods, repair of goods, reconditioning
of goods and technological/ Fashion upgrading of goods

2 **Junction 2 virgin materials v recycling materials**
Cost advantage virgin materials

Loop 2 recycling of materials

Source: W R Stahel and G Reday (1976/1981)

A CIRCULAR ECONOMY IS ABOUT MATERIAL AND RESOURCE SUFFICIENCY AND EFFICIENCY

This section presents new metrics to measure material efficiency, and quantifies the reductions in material consumption and emissions that can be achieved in the circular economy.

Stahel showed that many different types of innovation to increase material efficiency exist in the circular economy, including technical, commercial and 'utilisation' innovation. Technical innovation includes systems solution instead of product innovation (e.g. Plane Transport Systems).

A longer utilisation – long-life products, reuse and service-life extension of goods and components – are one option. A more intensive use of goods is another utilisation innovation to achieve a higher material efficiency, for instance through shared utilisation (together: public transport) or serial utilisation of goods (one after another: washing machines in laundromats and rental cars). These options need a 'new relationship with goods'; they were extensively discussed in the early 1990s but are only now finding a real interest on both the supply and demand side, for example in car-sharing initiatives.

Two distinctively different types of resource efficiency govern the circular economy: loop 1 in the graphic opposite is about resource sufficiency in the reuse and service-life extension of manufactured capital, loop 2 is about material efficiency in recycling materials (molecules).

The strategies of loop 1 are product specific – re-refining engine oil, solvents and other products with a catalytic function need a different approach from the service-life extension activities for buildings or mobile durable goods. The latter's resource efficiency can be improved by modular system design, component standardisation and other eco-design (design for environment) approaches which are now known and well documented.

The strategies of loop 2 are material specific – metals, ceramic materials and plastic use processes of physical and chemical recycling often derived from manufacturing processes, as well as new processes such as the depolymerisation of polymers. Materials with a low price/weight ratio, such as brick and concrete waste from demolishing buildings, are best crushed, using mobile equipment, for reuse as recycling concrete on-site for new constructions.

All materials come with a multiple backpack (rucksack) of mining waste and environmental impairment. These backpacks differ for each material and are highest for rare metals such as gold (with a backpack of 500,000), lowest for plastics (with a backpack of 0.1). Manufactured capital in the form of infrastructure, buildings, goods and components has individual accumulated backpacks of all the materials and energies they embed, which have to be calculated individually in a circular economy.

Manufactured capital contains, in addition to the backpacks of the materials it is made of, the sum of the embodied energy and greenhouse gases (GHG) emissions as well as the (virtual) water of the manufacturing steps from basic materials into finished goods and up to the point of sale. The reuse, remarketing and service-life extension activities in a circular economy preserve the mining backpacks of water and energy inputs and related GHG emissions in the manufacturing chain up to the point of sale, which are embodied in the finished goods. In addition, they also prevent the environmental impairment of the material recycling and/or waste management processes.

Higher resource efficiency also means reduced costs for material and energy procurement, as well as for waste disposal, waste water treatment and emissions.

A CIRCULAR ECONOMY IS ABOUT AN INTELLIGENT USE OF HUMAN LABOUR – JOB CREATION IN A REGIONAL ECONOMY

This section explains why human labour – work – is different from the other renewable resources: creative, versatile and adaptable, able to be educated but perishable if unused. The circular economy needs workers familiar with past technologies and thus offers jobs for 'silver workers'. "Roughly three-quarters of all industrial energy consumption is associated with the extraction or production of basic materials like steel and cement, while only about one-quarter is used in the transformation of raw material into finished goods such as machines and buildings. The converse is true of labour, about three times as much being used in the conversion of

materials to finished products as is required in the production
of material."

Compared to the traditional manufacturing process, the labour input of
the circular economy is higher as (a) its economies of scale are limited
in geographic and volume terms, and (b) remanufacturing comprises
additional steps of dismantling, cleaning and quality control, which are
absent in manufacturing.

No estimations exist on the impact of a circular economy on a
national labour market. Yet, employment is at the heart of the social
pillar of sustainability.

Furthermore, substituting labour for other resources is also an intelligent
solution for reasons which are inherent in human labour – it is the only
renewable resource with a qualitative characteristic. Work is the most
versatile and adaptable of all resources, with a strong but perishable
qualitative edge: (a) it is the only resource capable of creativity and
with the capacity to produce innovative solutions, and (b) human skills
deteriorate if unused – continuity of work and continued learning are
necessary to maintain skills and upgrade capabilities. A person who has
been unemployed for a few years risks becoming unemployable.

Governments should give priority to human labour in resource use
because a barrel of oil or a ton of coal left in the ground for another
decade will not deteriorate, nor will it demand social welfare, and
not taxing labour reduces incentives for black labour in the shadow
economy and thus reduces the costs for governments to monitor and
punish abuses.

A CIRCULAR ECONOMY IS ABOUT CARING

One of the objectives of a circular economy is to preserve the quality,
performance and value of the existing stock, wealth and welfare.
This certainly concerns manufactured capital, such as buildings,
infrastructure, equipment and goods is a key criteria if selling
performance (goods as services).

Stock management needs statistics and metrics to measure the
variations of wealth due to variations in the quality of stock. GDP is a
flow metric, ignoring whether our wealth – the stock – has increased as a

result of the flow. This situation has been compared to a bath tub where only the inflow of hot and cold water is measured, but the outflow and the water level are ignored.

Stock management includes people's skills, education and health, knowledge and know-how. Preserving culture is also linked to stock, not flow management; maintaining UNESCO world heritage sites, museums and examples of technological achievements will all profit from the shift in taxation towards the non-taxation of renewable resources. And caring is a high-quality world: Stradivari instruments and expensive watches do not live forever by design, but through periodic remanufacturing, motivated by caring.

Caring is a key characteristic of managing stock – caring for keeping up existing values and qualities. Most car owners will credit the manufacturer of their vehicle for its continued reliable functioning, rather than their mechanic who provides the maintenance and repair services. A change in popular values and beliefs would multiply the perception of caring as a pillar of the (circular) economy. The fleet of vintage and old-timer cars in the UK could be a point in case.

RETAINED OWNERSHIP OF GOODS AND EMBODIED MATERIAL PROVIDES FUTURE RESOURCE SECURITY

This section looks at why selling goods as service, or performance, is the most profitable and resource-efficient business model of the circular economy. By focussing on systems solutions, it internalises the cost of risk and of waste; by retaining the ownership of goods and the embodied resources, it creates a corporate and national resource security for the future.

Many economists have a problem accepting that this is a discontinuity in traditional economic business models, and look at the sale of performance as an extension of the aftermarket.

Economic actors retaining material ownership over the full life of their products gain a future resource security but accept a liability for the performance of their goods. Such a performance economy is based on the triple objectives of more growth and more jobs in combination with substantially reduced resource consumption. This triple objective can be achieved through three new business models: producing performance, selling performance and maintaining performance over time.

Success is measured using two new metrics in the form of absolute decoupling indicators: value per weight ($/kg) and labour-input per weight (man-hours/kg).

In the performance economy, providing materials services can be achieved, for instance, by building residential housing without capital. The developer rents all material and equipment from the manufacturers, say over a period of 50 years, who in return receive a yearly rent, financed by the rental income from the apartments. As the manufacturers have to give a 50-year guarantee for their material, they will make sure that the most appropriate material is used and applied correctly.

Selling performance differs according to the characteristics of products and is widely present in today's economy: selling goods as services by operating private and public networks (railways, telecom, motorways, airports); chemical management services and rent-a-molecule; energy management and integrated crop management services; rental and operational leasing of real estate; selling custom-made indoor climate for energy companies; private finance initiatives (known as PFIs) as a strategy to sell the utilisation of infrastructure according to the 'consumer pays principle', such as the French and Italian toll motorways; facility management of real estate and industrial plants; textile leasing (professional attire, hotel and hospital linen). These are but a few examples of the business model of selling performance, which also include rent-a-wash, rent-a-molecule and chemical leasing, as well as renting fashionable consumer goods (taking the waste out of fashion, see websites to rent ladies' handbags).

Selling performance is the most profitable and most material-efficient business model of the circular economy, as it is built on exploiting the small loops. It focuses on utilisation optimisation and exploits resource efficiency as well as sufficiency and prevention options to gain financial advantages and higher competitiveness. And it can be applied to all types of goods, see the table, on the next page.

Water and energy savings, as well as waste prevention, now become profitable activities that positively impact the financial bottom line of corporations. Whereas in the industrial economy, sufficiency and prevention options during the utilisation phase of goods present a loss of income, and are thus undesirable.

Selling performance, results, utilisation, services instead of goods means that economic actors:

a) retain the ownership of goods and embodied resources; and,

b) internalise the cost of risk and of waste.

By comparison, the industrial economy maximises its profit by externalising the cost of risk and of waste. After the point of sale, it offers a warranty for a limited period of time and limited to manufacturing defects.

By internalising the cost of risk and the cost of waste, economic actors selling performance have an economic incentive to prevent any future liability after the point of sale.

KEY BUSINESS STRATEGIES OF THE FUNCTIONAL SERVICE ECONOMY

Corporate strategies and product groups	S1 Prevention strategies	S2 Manufacturers selling performance, services or results	S3 Manufacturers Fleet managers with loop responsibility	S4 Fleet managers with maintenance & operation responsibility	R Independent remanufacturers
		SCIENCE			
Consumption goods (fuel)					
Dissipative goods (paint)	Knowledge-based solutions	Vertical integration	An economy in closed loops	Utilisation optimisation	Product-life extension
Catalytic goods (engine oil, solvents)					
Durable mobile goods (cars)					
Durable immobile goods (buildings)		EPeR Extended Performance Responsibility		JOBS Job creation potential	

Source: Stahel, W.R. 2010 The Performance Economy

Retaining ownership of their goods and embodied resources over the full life of their products gives corporations in times of rising resource prices (see next section) a high future resource security and resource price guarantee as well as a competitive cost advantage against throughput-based competitors, along the lines of: "The goods of today are the resources of tomorrow at yesterday's prices".

Buying performance is the demand side strategy equivalent to selling performance. Buying goods as services creates the same resource efficiency advantages and can be regarded as a new green public procurement policy. Buying services instead of hardware is the preferred procurement option of parts of the US administration, such as NASA and the Pentagon, and has sparked a number of innovative start-up companies. NASA now buys exclusively orbital services from companies such as Space-X; the space shuttle was the last NASA-owned and operated hardware to provide Earth orbit services.

Michelin provides tyre-use services to all parts of the US armed forces: for aircraft tyres, a fee per landing is charged; vehicle tyres pay a fixed fee per 100 miles. This service of 'pay by the mile' is now also offered to French and US fleet managers of lorries, using a business model of mobile tyre service workshops to make tyres last as long as safely possible. *http://www.michelintruck.com/michelintruck/services/ MichelinFleetSolutions.jsp*

POLICY FOR MATERIAL EFFICIENCY: THE ROLE OF SUSTAINABLE TAXATION AND SUSTAINABLE FRAMEWORK CONDITIONS
Sustainable framework conditions should treat the circular economy on its own merits, by:

a) Not taxing work – human labour as a zero-carbon renewable resource.
b) Not charging VAT on such value-preservation activities as reuse, repair and remanufacturing, with the possible exception of technologic upgrading activities. Major re-marketing activities, such as flea-markets and eBay, are already de facto exempt from VAT.
c) Giving carbon credits for the prevention of GHG emissions, not only for their reduction. The small loops (graphic on page 96) constitute a prevention of GHG emissions (and waste) but receive no carbon credits under any of the existing or planned GHG emission programmes, such as the Kyoto Protocol, which are based on the linear thinking of the industrial economy: first pollute, then reduce pollution to receive carbon credits.

Sustainable politics should build on simple and convincing principles, such as: Do not tax what you want to foster, punish unwanted effects instead. Also, it should promote sustainable solutions. Ideally, sustainable solutions create self-reinforcing virtuous circles, which guarantee their longevity.

Not taxing renewable resources, including work, and taxing non-renewable ones instead, creates virtuous self-reinforcing circles, by creating incentives to work more (no penalty for higher income) and by creating more wealth from less new resource input (increasing caring in resource use, including long-term resource ownership).
Sustainable taxation should reward desired developments and discourage unwanted effects of activities. In a sustainable economy, taxes on renewable resources, including work – human labour – are counterproductive and should be abandoned. The resulting loss of state revenue could be compensated by taxing the consumption of non-renewable resources in the form of materials and energies, and of undesired wastes and emissions. Such a shift in taxation would promote and reward a circular economy with its local low-carbon and low-resource solutions. These are inherently more labour-intensive than manufacturing because economies of scale in a circular economy are limited. Taxes on non-renewable resources could be charged in a similar way to today's Value Added Tax (VAT), also for imported goods.

The intelligent use of human labour has traditionally been discouraged through taxation, whereas the waste of it has been 'encouraged' in some industrialised countries through generous welfare. This shows that the role of work as a renewable resource in the economy has been misunderstood by policymakers.

SUMMARY
The linear industrial economy is best in overcoming situations of scarcity of food, goods, shelter. But in a situation of saturated markets, a circular economy is best suited to manage existing stock. In 1980, the market penetration for durable household goods in France was already above 90 percent for all social classes. In Germany, from 1995 onwards, the number of cars scrapped each year has been roughly the same as the number of cars newly registered. Continued production in saturated markets constitutes a substitution of, not an addition to, wealth, at the cost of "intensive and often inefficient use of resources".

For the last 100 years, resource prices for energy and material have constantly decreased; maintaining ownership of materials to assure access to future resources made little sense. At the beginning of the 21st century, this trend has changed, and it is expected that resource prices in the 21st century will constantly increase – a theory formulated by experts at the European Commission and prominently by the asset manager Jeremy Grantham who called it "the big paradigm shift".

Resource security could, therefore, become a major political bone of contention; and economic actors maintaining resource ownership will enjoy a certain guarantee of resource availability and price in the future, at the same time providing resource security for nations.

A sustainable tax policy of not taxing renewable resources, including work, constitutes a very powerful lever to accelerate, boost and generalise the circular economy and its positive impacts on resource security and regional job creation, while simultaneously reducing GHG emissions, as summarised in the figure below.

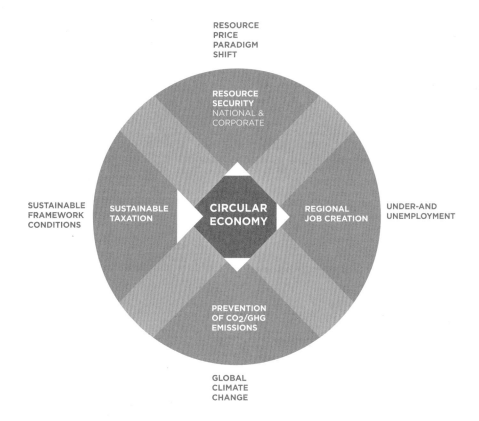

Sustainable taxation will promote the circular economy which in turn boosts resource security, regional job creation and the prevention of GHG emissions
Source: W R Stahel (2011)

Photo: Jocelyn Blériot

6 SOCIAL CAPITAL, MARKETS AND MONEY IN A CIRCULAR ECONOMY

The problems standing in the way of prosperity are an unsound ... money system and a lack of understanding of the physical reality underlying economics. What normally passes for economics is really the study of chrematistics. Chrematistics is the study of commerce, of wants and demands and of how they exchange for one another. Or simply put, the study of buying and selling.

Frederick Soddy
Wealth, Virtual Wealth, and Debt:
The Solution of the Economic Paradox (1926)

Frederick Soddy was writing in the 1920s, a Nobel laureate in chemistry who turned his attention to economics. He was the first to really try and embed the economy in materials and energy flows and understanding what money is, as opposed to just what it does.

His characterisation of chrematistics – it never caught on as a word, unsurprisingly – as a description of just one part of the economy still seems very useful. A circular economy is a study of the whole economy including the money system and the energetic and material resources upon which it is built. It is also a study of buying and selling, and so long as commerce is not confused with the economy, or the circular economy reduced to that state, then conversations will be systemic. If what has been said about systems is reasonable, then this will be 'a good thing'.

One of the suggested criteria for a functioning circular economy is that of effective markets allocating resources between competing ends. Economies are a complex interplay of materials, energy and information. Effective markets are key in the informational context. It is assumed that the rules under which markets operate are a social agreement of some kind and that thereafter freedom to make contracts, to have access to or leave these markets and the fair enforcement of the rules within the agreement, is appropriate.

If prices are messages between buyers and sellers, public and private, then ideally they should reveal the full costs if they, and the markets of which they are an expression, are to be effective. Markets are very much seen as arbiters in decisions about resources and the argument is that if they are not honest then they do not allocate resources rationally and their status is much diminished.

Unfortunately, distortions in markets are all too common, in fact the norm, and their ability to tell the truth is often compromised. Examined from the point of view of the circular economy – which emphasises the importance of effective (unhindered and adequate) flows for the 'health' of the whole system – two problem areas particularly stand out. Firstly, the effect of taxes on wages and salaries acting as a disincentive to using labour. The throughput economy supports the replacement of labour by technology (and cheap energy) by taxing income and writing off much capital depreciation in tax terms. But labour is a plentiful renewable resource: indeed, if not used, labour skills and confidence decline, and labour being overpriced slows the transition to a circular economy. Increasing employment and the substitution of capital by labour is often listed as a regionally significant benefit to a circular economy. Walter Stahel claims that a shift in taxation to non-renewables and waste is one of the key drivers for change (See Chapter 5). Taxes could focus on the non-renewable, on unearned income and on waste streams.

A second problem is so-called perverse subsidies. This is where non-renewables and stocks of natural capital (soils, fisheries, groundwater, forests) are exploited at prices which are below market levels and which probably already inadequately reflect the true value of the resources. The size of these subsidies is very significant globally. They are estimated at up to USD 1.1 trillion each year for resource consumption.[1] (This estimate refers only to direct cash payments to producers and so doesn't take into account other indirect support mechanisms including tax measures and other government interventions on prices received by producers and paid by consumers.) These subsidies encourage the wasteful use of resources while reducing the savings from investments to use the resources more efficiently. Simply eliminating the subsidies applied to the exploitation of many primary resources – in fossil fuels, mining, forestry, agriculture, fishing and banking – would enable prices better to reveal full costs.

Other distorting factors in the 'information' space include regulation and legislation which for example designate some materials 'waste' and deny access to them for some more positive potential uses (see opposite).

More significantly, in the economy as a whole, there is the need to create adequate returns for short-term financing or short-term shareholder interests. One paradox of the very successful linear economy has been increasing the share of the economic pie going to unearned income (economic rents) which in turn are in search of good returns on onward investment. The amounts involved are huge and the funds are volatile, always looking for that slightly better margin, which because of the large amounts involved is significant at fractions of a percentage point. Other examples of short-term activity include the volumes traded on the stock exchange and foreign exchange markets per day.

The opportunities for investment and financing in a circular economy will need to be visible: the existence of appreciating material assets (long-term trend) and rising energy prices (resource conserving activity) is indicative of the benefits of maintaining capital(s) long term. This would then point to the use of novel financial (informational) instruments which are consonant with the rebuilding and maintenance of productive capital. Peripheral change in this direction is the peer-to-peer lending like Zopa where lending on something which is less than 'optimal' from the traditional lender's perspective is quite acceptable. Crowd funding through the web-based Kickstarter and Indiegogo is another direct funding relationship.

SYSTEM BARRIERS, AN EXAMPLE

BBC Newsnight Investigation, 21 August 2013

 Chef Thomasina Miers wants to talk about food – not the food served up in her Mexican restaurant chain Wahaca – but the food fed to Britain's pigs.

Pigs are the most efficient converters of food waste to calories – we need calories in this world to feed growing populations – but in the meantime all pigs throughout Europe are being fed soya which is being grown in the Amazon basin.

"...man and pig have been living in perfect harmony and synergy for thousands of years," she says. Man creates waste; pig eats waste and turns it into food that we eat again. It is a perfect circle which means food has a use.

Feeding catering waste to pigs has been banned across the European Union since 2003.

BBC 21 August 2013

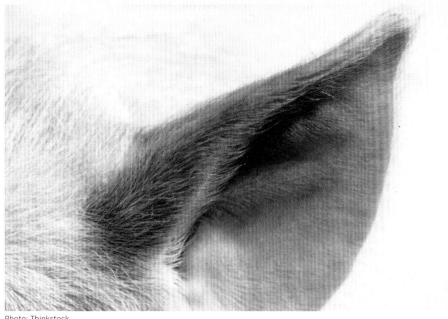

Photo: Thinkstock

Almost all existing money flows are based on a kind of monetary monoculture – with the interchangeability of euros, US dollars, pounds, yen and Swiss Francs for example – and if the major operators in these currencies are disinclined to get involved in the physical processes of restoring capital and working on the longer term then change seems overdue. Or put another way, if financial economics works in one direction and a putative circular economy in the opposite what results? If it is true that the financial system had a lot to do with the building of the economy – by creating and advancing credit before production takes place – then it is a parent of the economy. Money is an active part of the economic model rather than outside of it.

What an injection of credit started can quickly go into reverse if economic growth – the means to pay off loans and interest – falters or stalls. Therefore in a responsible role it would be a self-interested position for the financial system to channel significant investment into the transition towards the circular economy if that is the best chance to maintain economic growth. The financial system then becomes the icing on the cake of the economy writ large (see diagram opposite).

The financial system needs the productive economy to underwrite its existence and, in turn the productive economy rests on the societal (informal) economy and, finally, a resource and ecosystems services base. Optimising the system means recognising and working with these interdependencies in the end.

Another complementary approach is to get some diversity into the financial money system. Money circuits are all pretty much short term and detached from the productive side of the economy except that underlying asset values are pumped up and firms become concerned about share prices and quarterly results – and governments about debt. There is a money shortage in effect.

This does not help the circular economy which is looking longer term to rebuild capital (natural and social) in order to design out waste and make many more, and more varied, productive flows 'work' for enterprise. These are not flows which typically attract financial capital and are hard to make work when demands for returns are short term and at interest.

ECONOMY AS A THREE-LAYERED CAKE (WITH ICING)

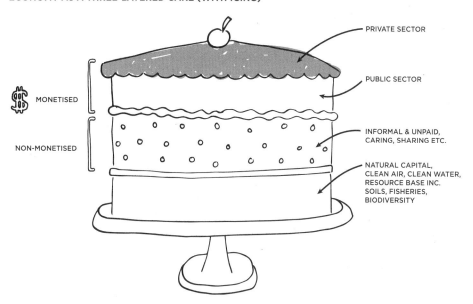

PRIVATE SECTOR

PUBLIC SECTOR

MONETISED

NON-MONETISED

INFORMAL & UNPAID, CARING, SHARING ETC.

NATURAL CAPITAL, CLEAN AIR, CLEAN WATER, RESOURCE BASE INC. SOILS, FISHERIES, BIODIVERSITY

It is worth noting that the most recent trends mean that the 'non-monetised' layer of the cake has shrunk with the advent of peer-to-peer exchanges (fee-based car sharing and private accommodation being offered to paying guests etc). If this 1991 drawing was to be re-sketched today, its shape would reflect that evolution.

Adapted from Hazel Henderson, *Paradigms in progress* (1991)

The lack of adequate 'monocultural' money flows clearly applies to some categories of materials, particularly low-value 'waste' streams. Since the current money monoculture is not serving circularity particularly well, one answer is to sidestep it and create other money circuits. It is invoking the circular economy principle that diversity = strength so the use of, for example, complementary business-to-business currencies can be seen as a way of unblocking flows or extending them.

A so-called 'complementary currency' sits alongside the official currency; it is a pure means of exchange and is not subject to the same speculation, interest rates etc as official currencies. Specific complementary currencies can energise circuits in materials flows which are circular but not necessarily properly valorised or enabled using the monoculture currency. In this way circularity is enhanced markedly, especially if positive interest is avoided and taxes can be paid in this currency. The fit between innovations in currencies and funding, the need to give value to hitherto neglected materials flows and to invest in resources *longer term,* which so much characterises the circular economy, is another welcome synergy.

Complementary currencies can be tied to community gardening and food production (see the Torekes[2] in Ghent) or to spent brewery grains, chicken manure, or more generally, as is the case with the Bristol Pound.

The UK's first city-wide complementary currency: the Bristol Pound.
Launched in autumn 2012. Paper based and via TXT2PAY. Local taxes
can be part paid in Bristol Pounds.
Photo: London News Pictures/Rex

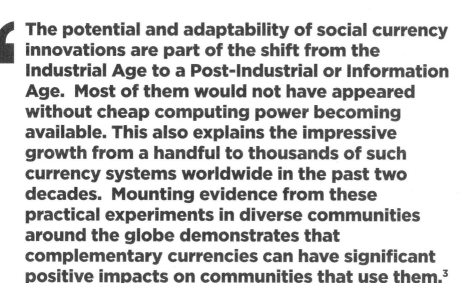

The potential and adaptability of social currency innovations are part of the shift from the Industrial Age to a Post-Industrial or Information Age. Most of them would not have appeared without cheap computing power becoming available. This also explains the impressive growth from a handful to thousands of such currency systems worldwide in the past two decades. Mounting evidence from these practical experiments in diverse communities around the globe demonstrates that complementary currencies can have significant positive impacts on communities that use them.[3]

Peer-to-peer payments between mobiles are becoming commonplace in a few countries – the M Pesa in Kenya is an example. Sixty per cent of Kenyans now use their mobile phone for banking transactions and 64% of Kenyans send or receive money locally through their mobile phones, according to a study by the Kenya Bankers Association.[4] In Afghanistan a peer-to-peer payment of police salaries revealed huge corruption in the earlier system of cash payments and helped rebuild confidence – a form of social capital of course.

BUSINESS-TO-BUSINESS COMPLEMENTARY CURRENCY

Imagine grain is sold in the normal way to a brewery. It makes use of the grain but 80% of the physical material is still existent at the end of the brewing process, but this has a low value conventionally speaking.

Introduce a brewery feedstock waste currency. The brewery now has a product for sale in, let's call it, 'Points'. A mushroom grower buys the spent grains with Points and knows that the bio-substrate left after mushroom growing on it can also be sold, in 'Points' (the mushrooms are sold conventionally). Then the substrate is used by another farmer as a soil improver to fertilise and rebuild soils. The burying of such bio-substrate in excess of what this other farmer needs to produce a crop like last year (the capital formation) can be offset against taxes. All along the chain, taxes can be paid in Points to some degree so that the creation of the 'Points' is extinguished ready for another cycle. Thus a business-to-business complementary currency eases and encourages these material flows, and its circulation is ensuring that the soils are rebuilt – rebuilding capital.

Person-to-person loans or crowd funding through the web-based Kickstarter or Indiegogo are doing the job of bringing the economy down to the individual and community once more by lowering barriers to access. Surely it matters what the project is about if it is a part of a circular economy. But a circular economy is a description of a more free-flowing, effective economy where materials energy and information are more abundant. Finance is a part of that, as is innovation, as is working at multiple scales. A linear economy has centralising characteristics – a circular economy has distributive ones – at least that is the aspiration. And with all this access to tools, to materials, to each other and the freeing up of education, money and finance, this abundance succours participation and it succours democracy. A circular economy is not primarily about technical materials and recycling/recovering them while moving to renewables. It is a different way to see the economy which includes the material but is not limited by it.

In a circular economy materials can cycle in either pathway – biological or technical – and will return to increase, or at least maintain, the natural and perhaps social capital upon which long-term prosperity depends. It is that 'perhaps' which exercises some people most. What does the circular economy imply for the social capital side of the economy?

Social capital is a representation of what resources reside in the relationships between people in various communities. Social capital is those non-money exchanges and mutualities which so enrich our lives and weave some of the fabric of what we term civilisation. Civilisation is based, after all, on the word 'civis' or citizen, but set in a collective context of other citizens. We create civilisation by participating and routinely contrast it with anarchy (no order) or tyranny (no freedom). Civilisation is a form of ordered complexity. It is what we value the most and yet find so easy to destroy.

A circular economy, drawing from living system analogies for its rationale, creates wealth by creating effective flows and maintaining or increasing capital. These flows are distributed across the scale because it is a condition of being resilient: too much efficiency brings brittleness, and too little, stagnation. This increased wealth that has been created may well translate into more employment in some sectors – although the effects of the drive for efficiency continue to dislodge employment elsewhere. But other changes are in play and these relate to the use of assets and the general trend towards a devolved economy. As described in Chapter 8, information technology, which has enabled both sharing and circular materials flows, has been a key to building social capital in new guises.

A circular economy sits well with the performance economy and as Walter Stahel has pointed out extended product life and the loops of maintenance, repair, refurbishment etc. are potentially profitable activities. As Chapter 7 illustrates, the sharing economy is about putting users and assets into a more effective relationship. So many assets are underused and so many new relationships can be and have been created amongst people through social networks like eBay, Freecycle, Airbnb or couch surfing. This rebuilding of social relationship is said to be a prime motivator, at least for many people involved in these IT-based networks.

Economies are in transition, and young people bridge the traditional and modern while bringing their own distinctive perceptions but it is access to a global communications, not just physical resources, that will accelerate transition quickly and play a role in enhancing social capital.

Information technology is central to finding markets for niche and local products or materials, aggregating small suppliers to meet demand and controlling variables – in food growing, in manufacturing and distribution. It is enabling small-scale businesses with a global presence, small-scale renewables with better returns, accessing assets, enabling sharing and rebuilding community relationships. IT is also enabling exchange and new funding sources. Social capital is built through interaction and these tools create networks in novel ways.

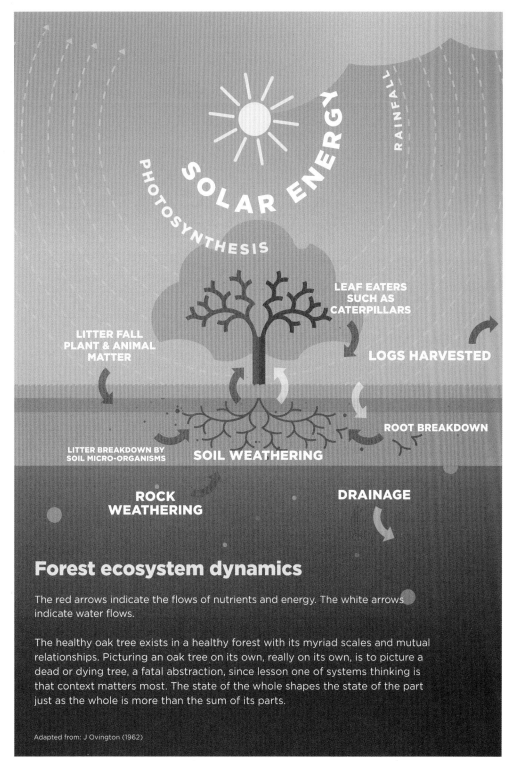

Forest ecosystem dynamics

The red arrows indicate the flows of nutrients and energy. The white arrows indicate water flows.

The healthy oak tree exists in a healthy forest with its myriad scales and mutual relationships. Picturing an oak tree on its own, really on its own, is to picture a dead or dying tree, a fatal abstraction, since lesson one of systems thinking is that context matters most. The state of the whole shapes the state of the part just as the whole is more than the sum of its parts.

Adapted from: J Ovington (1962)

Human adaptability and resilience in full flow.

After the financial crash... an improvised wedding venue in Greece.

Photo: Nick Hannes www.nickhannes.be

It would be deeply ironic if a circular economy, based on systems science, were to cower in the bunker of the technical cycle and reverse logistics and the role of IT being a puzzle around how to disassemble a server or a smart phone.

So there is a part of what a full circular economy is about which speaks to the notion of the value, and perhaps inevitability, of a more devolved economy that builds social capital – a thriving, regenerative economy that literally revitalises the underemployed resources, networks and poor neighbourhoods. It acheives this by emphasising tighter loops – maintenance, refurbishment, repair, a shift to services (customer/ user care) – as well as the provision of access to assets on a use, not ownership, basis. It sounds contemporary but it isn't – allotments were always a great idea, but belonged to a more communal era – now, with added self-created spending power (complementary currencies) and more emphasis on capturing waste as food and thinking creatively and entrepreneurially it's a different world. It all used to be a lot easier when existing social capital was based on shared factories, walkable and shared public spaces and extended families but, after their decline, it may fall to information technology and human ingenuity and imagination to be the most important tools for rebuilding social capital.

The circular economy does not have any political bias or ideological agenda. It is a model that offers to play with economic levers that will have an impact on the way society, and to a certain extent globalisation, are shaped and operate. Yet this does not mean that it contains organisational preconceptions or dogmatic frameworks. But what the model of the circular economy *implies* is that increased prosperity can come from circularity, from stock maintenance and additional flows. Walter Stahel talks of caring in his essay (Chapter 5). It is an economy that assumes that being more productive and enabling more production in the positive sense of the 'upcycle', as described by Michael Braungart

| TAXI | PICK UP | DELIVERY | ASSISTANCE | VENDOR | SECURITY | RENTAL |

The signs on the small van describe the services it supports: Taxi; Pick-up; Delivery; Assistance; Vendor; Security; Rental.

Seven functions, one vehicle. As imagined in a project in Belgium called Mobilotoop[5] the van, when coupled with a pay-per-use leasing framework, and radically distributed computing, becomes an element within an asset-light mobility ecosystem.

Mobilotoop asks, "how will we move in the city of the future?" 'Cloud commuting' in this context, is about accessing the means to move when needed (such as the micro-van, below) rather than owning a large heavy vehicle that will sit unused for 95% of the time.

The first cross-over project of Design Platform Vlaanderen, this two-year research project focuses on potential connections between people, vehicles, places and services that – as a single ecosystem – generates new mobility solutions dynamically, and continuously.

Until now, we've moved ourselves – and stuff – about the city in ridiculously wasteful ways. A snapshot from The Netherlands: 1,900 vans and trucks enter the small city of Breda each day, 90% of those deliveries could be done by bike, or e-bike. Once all system costs are included, a cargo cycle can be up to 98% cheaper per km than four-wheeled, motorised alternatives.[6]

Mobile media, flexible vehicle designs, and adaptive infrastructure enable everyone to be a user and a supplier of mobility services. Every commuter can deliver a package on her way to work.[7]

Photo: CargoCab.
Concept / design: Thomas Lommée / Intrastructures
Courtesy Intrastructures

and William McDonough, is 'a good thing'. Implied in the idea of prospering *long term* and taking insights from living systems is an economy which works at *all* scales and provides multiple benefits from restoring natural and social capital.

Hyde Park tollgate

The IT revolution is enabling circularity and the rethinking of materials, energy and credit flows. It is also one key to rebuilding social capital, social networks. It has lowered barriers to access to the tools of self-reliance and community building and has opened up new possibilities for operating on a variety of scales and in new competitive or collaborative combinations. In money and finance, energy, manufacturing, materials use, design, education, creative arts, communications, urban food production: it's all changing. The net result can be lowered energy thresholds, effective materials flows, easy and affordable access to assets and tools of all kinds. The promise is of abundance not scarcity. It is not so much a case of challenging existing linear businesses – like centralised large-scale fossil fuel-based utilities – as doing an end run around them and growing from there.

All is not necessarily rosy. Rescuing underutilised renewable resources, especially labour, can be counterpointed with the use of information technologies to control a flow and extract rent from it. An analogy is the tollbooth, where traditionally access to a road was controlled and charged in excess of that required to maintain the asset. 'Rent-seeking' opportunities could arise if certain materials were able to be tracked and recovered and the market dominated by few suppliers. Such materials would become a new asset class. Other examples include restricted access to certain professions in order to keep income high, excessive copyright and IP restrictions or keeping buildings unused to protect rental values.

A circular economy may be an economy that favours the 'makers' not the 'takers', based on Michael Lind's observations[8] about the USA where he sees that the existing situation favours rent seekers (takers) rather than profit-seeking entrepreneurs in the industrial economy (makers).

In contrast to the tollbooth analogy, a circular economy has more of the lighthouse about it – the asset is available and at no or low cost to the user. An iconic example of course, but one that has a useful resonance even in the era of global positioning systems.

St Catherine's lighthouse, Isle of Wight
Photo: Jocelyn Blériot

Photo: Jocelyn Blériot

7 THE SHARING ECONOMY

"Sharing economy business models emerge from our oldest instincts as humans – cooperation, sharing, generosity, individual choice and flexibility. Models include renting, bartering, loaning, gifting, swapping and forms of shared ownership such as cooperative structures. Many of the most popular models are based on what is called a 'two-sided market' which is a market where an information technology-enabled platform is developed, built and maintained by a third party but the function of the platform is to enable sharing economy activities. Most sharing economy structures are enabled by new technologies of connection."
Wikipedia: Collaborative Consumption

In the last part of Chapter 6 the key to the rise of the circular economy was said to turn on the coming together of a number of technologies and trends. Some are opportunities, some are threats. In the economy writ large, and by that is meant the economy as it relates to energy, materials and information, not just financials, the first two trends are upward movement in materials costs and price volatility. The same trend applies to energy, especially oil and coal. As recently as the year 2005, oil was USD 43 a barrel,[1] copper USD 3,170/mt,[2] and indium USD 850/kg.[3] Coal (US) was USD 67 per tonne.[4] The graphs opposite show the trends for all the movements for copper and oil.

COPPER (2005–14)
UNITS: USD/MT

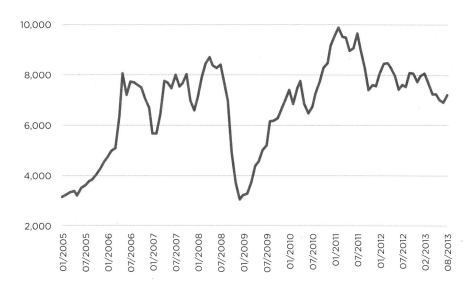

CRUDE OIL, AVERAGE (2005–14)
UNITS ARE: USD/BBL

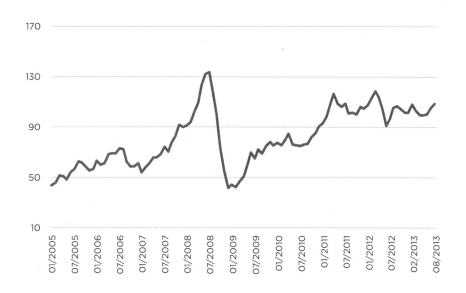

The fourth trend is the end of cheap and easy credit. Since the mid-1970s wages and salaries as a share of the economic pie (see page 41) in the developed world have been pretty fixed while productivity soared. The results of this stagnation were that not all that was produced was able to be bought by workers with declining savings without the liberal availability of credit. Even so, the returns to manufacturing *per se* declined as overproduction took hold. The problem was no longer how much it cost to make sports shoes, but how much it cost to market it successfully in saturated consumed-out markets demanding novelty, brand and shopping experience. As we know, this credit expansion was curtailed in 2007/8 and the consequences of this downturn have not been resolved despite upticks in financials and assets in the last few years.

Overproduction, inadequate credit, expensive materials and energy, rising unemployment and falling public spending (not to mention massive increases in the middle class in Asia) spell change. Business as usual looks like a radical's manifesto. It is also a part answer to those who ask 'why would I vote for a sharing or circular economy?' – Why would you vote for a linear one?

Meanwhile, information technology has allowed us to increasingly track 'stuff' and its use. This might be raw materials but it might be infrastructure. It might be buses and trains and taxis or it might be the legacy of a hundred-odd years of stuff, the assets on the ground and under the ground, in our cities and towns and suburbs. IT also allows us to track each other, since there are more mobile phone accounts than toilets on the planet. Not only is stuff now connected to us – there is an app for that! – it is increasingly connected to other stuff, the internet of things: where fridges adjust their cycling to energy price information, where aero engines monitor themselves and schedule their own maintenance[5] and where (electric) cars store electricity from the grid in their lithium batteries. And connection is increasingly about *now*: where fishing catches are sold as they are hauled up from the sea or where Uber lets you summon a classy taxi ride from your smart phone on the street corner with the press of a button. All paperwork waived.

In finance, there is the crowd funding, the Kickstarter and Indiegogo, plus the Zopa peer-to-peer lending (see also Chapter 6). In design there are the open source arrangements and crowd sourcing and collaborative everything, even manufacturing, from rapid prototyping through 3D printing, laser and water cutters, to hacking of components and subassemblies for repurpose (see Chapter 8). In the industrialised world it feels as if mass production was so very linear-economy, so very much of its time. All the rest is bound for the circular where custom experiences, quality of life and access over ownership is not only acceptable but desirable, easier and could be cheaper. And profitable. Perhaps even necessary post-2008 and the Great Recession.

The human and business energy behind the information technology-driven 'sharing economy' helps save money, helps create new income flows from assets heavily underutilised and provides a speculative bubble all of its own in societies with too much money chasing too few returns. However, the sharing economy has to do much more. It has to fit seamlessly with the physical and energetic 'rules of the game' of the circular economy so as to create a positive cycle of development which restores natural capital as well as social capital. In doing both of these, the sharing economy stands a chance of thriving in the long term.

The basics of circularity are very easy. Materials are of two types ideally: those which are consumed and rebuilt through the biosphere safely – biological materials or 'nutrients', and those which cycle at high quality for longer in the technical nutrients cycle (as products primarily, providing services, the main focus for 'access over ownership' of course). What point is there in having complex plastics or alloys, however 'shared', if they are only capable of downcycling – detouring to the dump through reduced quality – or being completely trashed as not worth the reprocessing? The sharing economy is not for the long term if materials losses are ignored and merely pushed off into the future. So the emphasis is on design, as always. The sharing economy must fit a circular economy by intention, not happenstance. It needs to address design for disassembly (which also means easy repair, upgrade, and finally disposal). The sharing economy must also consider design for waste = food materials pathways, so that new income streams and ingenuity can apply here too, and less new material is required. In the producer value chain, the highest energy and materials costs are in mining and manufacturing so the sharing economy gets a plus for contributing to extended product use. With effective materials cycles, energy costs keep falling and the threshold to using renewables becomes lower – and being more localised and labour intensive, additional jobs are created. At least for a time.

Many proponents of the sharing economy point out that it is building, or rebuilding, a sense of community. It is therefore rebuilding social capital and encouraging innovation and entrepreneurship. But if it can also work on the biological materials side, particularly, to rebuild natural capital (soils, forests, fisheries and associated ecosystem services) then it will allow more production and consumption overall. Increased natural capital then leads to increased flows.

LANDSHARE

It began with the tiny seed of an idea – and it's growing and growing.

Landshare brings together people who have a passion for home-grown food, connecting those who have land to share with those who need land for cultivating food. Since its launch through River Cottage in 2009 it has grown into a thriving community of more than 55,000 growers, sharers and helpers.

It's for people who:

Want to grow their own fruit and veg but don't have anywhere to do it

Have a spare bit of land they're prepared to share

Can help in some way – from sharing knowledge and lending tools to helping out on the plot itself

Support the idea of freeing up more land for growing

Bangladeshi women teach a community group in Bradford (UK) about vegetable growing

Photo: Photofusion/Rex

It will be noticeable that the idea of limiting consumption and production as an aesthetic does not feature in a circular economy model *per se*, since if all production and consumption is 'doing good' rather than an exercise in 'doing less harm' – and it is increasingly powered by renewables – then stuff is not a problem. Discussing 'stuff' doesn't need to come from some kind of moral standpoint. However, GDP – as we measure it now – could be undermined as we do more for ourselves and enjoy extended use periods and fuller use of assets and begin to eradicate waste. This really says more about the bias in the measure of GDP towards throughput than anything more profound. It would be absurd to adjust the economy to an increasingly inadequate metric. If polity and the public are fixated on GDP going up, then a sharing and circular economy could bring slower growth in the traditional sense or even falls, but if the measure of progress integrates 'well-being' or something more *considered* then the picture brightens considerably.

US GROSS PRODUCTION vs GENUINE PROGRESS 1960–2004

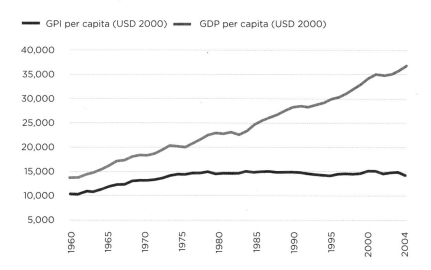

There is a long history of experiments with more rounded measures of economic activity. The Genuine Progress Indicator vs GDP: GPI nets figures that represent the cost of the negative effects related to economic activity (such as the cost of crime, cost of ozone depletion and cost of resource depletion, among others).

Source: Genuine Progress Indicator/Centre for Sustainable Economy

The harnessing of these materials flows across the various scales of the economy means that a sharing economy at the local and small scale could become more profitable not only due to the use of information and communications technology but as a consequence of the impacts on reduced transport, industrial (fossil fuel-based) agriculture and on centralised food processing. This then doubly reinforces the value of local or regional production and consumption. An example is the rise of urban agriculture including rooftop and daylight-less interior hydroponic systems, as well as the more traditional allotments. Small players are beginning to access their potential customers directly or by using aggregators (people who bring together small-scale producers and products and deliver sufficient scale for the bigger players). No doubt there are several 'apps' for this already.

> **Last night 40,000 people rented accommodation from a service that offers 250,000 rooms in 30,000 cities in 192 countries.**

The sharing economy also brings into focus the more complete valuing of materials, products or what were formerly simply waste streams. From Freecycle to eBay, this stuff can find a market now at low transaction costs. But, as Bartercard and other various complementary currencies have shown, this market can be *creatively extended*. As we saw in Chapter 6, money is primarily a matter of social agreement: it's one of our greatest inventions. Money is needed to facilitate exchange primarily and there is no need for a monopolistic money system, nor to have banks as the only lending institution. This is evidenced by the rise in complementary currencies and in peer-to-peer lending. Sharing in a circular economy? Well, the clue is of course in the name. Alongside rebuilt capital, in a circular economy there need to be effective flows and the use of complementary currencies can be directed at freeing up blockages in the flow of materials, products or services not well served by existing arrangements. It could be complementary currency for brewers' spent grains (see page 116) or for education: the principle is one of enabling effective exchange and therefore flows. To have a flow requires capital and in the monetary sphere this is credit. The aim, as always, is abundance not shortage.

ON THE INTERNET, EVERYTHING IS FOR HIRE

Last night 40,000 people rented accommodation from a service that offers 250,000 rooms in 30,000 cities in 192 countries. They chose their rooms and paid for everything online. But their beds were provided by private individuals, rather than a hotel chain. Hosts and guests were matched up by Airbnb, a firm based in San Francisco. Since its launch in 2008 more than 4m people have used it – 2.5m of them in 2012 alone. It is the most prominent example of a huge new sharing economy, in which people rent beds, cars, boats and other assets directly from each other, coordinated via the internet.

You might think this is no different from running a bed-and-breakfast, owning a timeshare or participating in a car pool. But technology has reduced transaction costs, making sharing assets cheaper and easier than ever – and therefore possible on a much larger scale. The big change is the availability of more data about people and things, which allows physical assets to be disaggregated and consumed as services. Before the Internet, renting a surfboard, a power tool or a parking space from someone else was feasible, but was usually more trouble than it was worth. Now websites such as Airbnb, RelayRides and SnapGoods match up owners and renters; smartphones with GPS let people see where the nearest rentable car is parked; social networks provide a way to check up on people and build trust; and online payment systems handle the billing.

Just as peer-to-peer businesses like eBay allow anyone to become a retailer, sharing sites let individuals act as an ad hoc taxi service, car-hire firm or boutique hotel as and when it suits them. Just go online or download an app. The model works for items that are expensive to buy and are widely owned by people who do not make full use of them. Bedrooms and cars are the most obvious examples, but you can also rent camping spaces in Sweden, fields in Australia and washing machines in France. As proponents of the sharing economy like to put it, access trumps ownership.

Rachel Botsman, the author of a book on the subject, says the consumer peer-to-peer rental market alone is worth USD 26 billion. Broader definitions of the sharing economy include peer-to-peer lending (though cash is hardly a spare fixed asset) or putting a solar panel on your roof and selling power back to the grid (though that looks a bit like becoming a utility). And it is not just individuals: the web makes it easier for companies to rent out spare offices and idle machines, too. But the core of the sharing economy is people renting things from each other.

....this 'collaborative consumption' is a good thing for several reasons. Owners make money from underused assets. Airbnb says hosts in San Francisco who rent out their homes do so for an average of 58 nights a year, making USD 9,300. Car owners who rent their vehicles to others using RelayRides make an average of USD 250 a month; some make more than USD 1,000. Renters, meanwhile, pay less than they would if they bought the item themselves, or turned to a traditional provider such as a hotel or car-hire firm. (It is not surprising that many sharing firms got going during the financial crisis.) And there are environmental benefits, too: renting a car when you need it, rather than owning one, means fewer cars are required and fewer resources must be devoted to making them.

For sociable souls, meeting new people by staying in their homes is part of the charm. Curmudgeons who imagine that every renter is Norman Bates can still stay at conventional hotels. For others, the web fosters trust. As well as the background checks carried out by platform owners, online reviews and ratings are usually posted by both parties to each transaction, which makes it easy to spot lousy drivers, bathrobe-pilferers and surfboard-wreckers. ...

PEERING INTO THE FUTURE

The sharing economy is a little like online shopping, which started in America 15 years ago. At first, people were worried about security. But having made a successful purchase from, say, Amazon, they felt safe buying elsewhere. Similarly, using Airbnb or a car-hire service for the first time encourages people to try other offerings. Next, consider eBay. Having started out as a peer-to-peer marketplace, it is now dominated by professional power sellers (many of whom started out as ordinary eBay users). The same may happen with the sharing economy, which also provides new opportunities for enterprise. Some people have bought cars solely to rent them out, for example.

Incumbents are getting involved too. Avis, a car-hire firm, bought a share in ZipCar, a car sharing rival. So do GM and Daimler, two carmakers. In the future, companies may develop hybrid models, listing excess capacity (whether vehicles, equipment or office space) on peer-to-peer rental sites. In the past, new ways of doing things online have not displaced the old ways entirely. But they have often changed them. Just as internet shopping forced Walmart and Tesco to adapt, so online sharing will shake up transport, tourism, equipment-hire and more.

A major worry is regulatory uncertainty... Will room-renters be subject to hotel taxes, for example? In Amsterdam officials are using Airbnb listings to track down unlicensed hotels. In some American cities, peer-to-peer taxi services have been banned after lobbying by traditional taxi firms. The danger is that although some rules need to be updated to protect consumers from harm, incumbents will try to destroy competition. People who rent out rooms should pay tax, of course, but they should not be regulated like a Ritz-Carlton hotel. The lighter rules that typically govern bed-and-breakfast establishments, it is argued, are more than adequate.

The sharing economy is the latest example of the internet's value to consumers. This emerging model is now big and disruptive enough for regulators and companies to have woken up to it. That is a sign of its immense potential. It is time to start caring about sharing.

© *The Economist* Newspaper Limited, London (2013)[6]

The general sense of rebuilding capitals (social, natural and financial), making effective flows of services or cascading materials through the systems to provide value at all scales, benefits from at least one fairly recent development which is valued by many advocates of circular and sharing alike. This is a systems worldview. The emphasis on feedback, access over ownership, the interaction of the parts not the parts themselves, the multiple and complex interdependencies, the valuing of all flows, the notions of open source, crowd funding, social networks, even the idea of 'pop-up' stores and other transient events speaks of fluidity and feedback within a complex and dynamic system. The sharing economy for many is primarily a revival in a new guise of the social capital building of neighbourhood and community.

The earlier Enlightenment 1.0 view was of a machine-like world of fixed relationships, of understand, predict and control. With it came standardisation, mass societies, mass production and individual ownership, of broadcast media and schooling by transmission ("sit up, lad, and listen"). This is being overthrown – intellectually by the recognition in the age of computing that most real world systems are non-linear, full of feedback. These systems reveal ordered complexity, not predictable results, that in human terms everyone contributes to and everyone can and does have an effect on them.

Perhaps through the sharing economy we are beginning to accept uncertainty, make arrangements based on transience and travelling light. Perhaps this in turn just mirrors the economic uncertainties, a way of adapting in a world where the prospect of regular, full-time, well-compensated, long-term work is fading for the majority.

In the complementarity of sharing and circular there exists this overarching sense of the dynamic system in its contemporary understanding – systems thinking. It brings both comfort and inspiration. This IS the way things work. In the circular economy the notion of insights from living systems is particularly important as they are perhaps the most refined of all non-linear systems groups.

One thing about systems approaches is that they are not grounded in direct, detailed interference. Yes, some products or materials might be arbitrarily prohibited or highly regulated – narcotics or fissile materials come to mind – but William McDonough argues that regulation is often just an attempt to compensate for, or limit the consequences of, poor and inadequate design.

Instead think of products embedded in enabling systems, where 'everything is food.' An analogy is a garden where nurturing, weeding and seeding might be the essential activities but the basic rules around the interaction of the parts, the rules of the game, if you like, are the real enablers.

Whether a large established firm or an insurgent start-up based in the agile digital domain, changing the business models appears to be the key. Adapting a business to 'roundput' is the touchstone for success even while the environment is unsettled, possibly hostile to it. Its success might also be part of rising expectations that more people can find a productive place in a circular economy than a linear. More people can participate not least because a sharing economy and designing for the full cycle of product and materials life means cooperation as well as competition. If there is no 'away' in circular economy – as in throwing things away – there is no exclusion either.

Jocelyn Blériot adds a note of caution: the whole model of sharing / renting – with communications channels included – makes a lot of sense. One can see its potential ... provided it's taken seriously enough to reach critical mass and become a second nature for wrongly named 'consumers'. To put things a bit bluntly, passing on a disused hair dryer on Freecycle and subsequently boasting about having embraced the 'collaborative consumption' philosophy at a dinner party simply will not do. Also, despite the obvious logic of that model there are psychological hurdles linked to ownership that need to be dealt with. Our relationship with objects is not always merely a utilitarian one, and as philosopher Jean Baudrillard pointed out in *The system of objects* (published in 1968) there is a strong symbolism to be taken into account as well. Developing this idea, he went on to examine our model in *The consumer society: myths and structure* in 1970 – his analysis was groundbreaking at the time, and a lot of his observations still stand today.

Collaborative consumption is a fast-developing movement offering tangible positive perspectives. But for it to really make a difference we must all challenge our own preconceptions and sometimes force our nature, because there are specific objects we're not ready to let go of. Some of these objects act as flags, they place us socially and send out messages about our personality, set of values and priorities. Or we hold on simply because we have a strong bond with them. But there are ways around this obstacle, which has to be taken into account but not seen as a brick wall. Granted, collaborative consumption does not mean that we should not own anything, but let's try and maximise its impact – as an individual, that could well mean determining a strict list of 'ring-fenced possessions'. By doing so, it's quite easy to identify the superfluous purchases in our lives – the word 'purchases' is crucial here, because the idea is not to move towards an austere lifestyle but to switch from owning goods to benefiting from the service they provide.

In that capacity, collaborative consumption and take-back systems seem to form a very effective combination: what I can live without on a daily basis I can source from collaborative networks when the need arises; and what I have to have (say a fridge, computer, a bicycle for the ones who cycle to work...) can be owned by the manufacturer. Both models work towards reducing or eradicating waste and safeguarding precious materials. It's easy to see the benefits of their large-scale implementation but it will not be without a conscious effort on the part of us 'consumers' notably because – and it would be intellectually dishonest to overlook this issue – the current market efforts are directed towards making sure we remain buyers. As Jean Baudrillard would have put it, the "ideological genesis of needs" is the driving force, which manifests itself in the form of TV advertising, marketing or credit... There is a lot of potential in the collaborative consumption idea, but it will have to avoid the trap into which 'traditional' recycling fell – in other words, becoming an alibi to carry on doing business as usual with a lighter conscience.

Photo: Berlin Wall. Jocelyn Blériot

8 DEVOLVED, DIGITAL AND OPEN SOURCE MANUFACTURING AND THE RISE OF URBAN MINING

"Three-dimensional printing makes it as cheap to create single items as it is to produce thousands and thus undermines economies of scale. It may have as profound an impact on the world as the coming of the factory did ... Just as nobody could have predicted the impact of the steam engine in 1750 – or the printing press in 1450, or the transistor in 1950 – it is impossible to foresee the long-term impact of 3D printing. But the technology is coming, and it is likely to disrupt every field it touches." *The Economist* (10th February 2011)

Reimagining the world of materials and products. What if it was based less on throughput and huge economies of scale, but more on carefully chosen materials, which are produced, used and re-made in more devolved regional and local economies?

Recycling, the recovery of materials at the end of life, can act as reinforcement for a linear economy because it is the only one of the four 'R's' (Rethink, Reduce, Reuse, Recycle) to have no real effect on existing consumption patterns. Recycling is also wasteful as it usually involves the loss of embedded energy and quality. In a circular economy, this might not be a problem if materials are designed well – to fit biological or technical material pathways – and the recovery of the technical materials is approaching 100%. It's a tough call though progress is being made.[1]

It is not just the end of life where losses occur. Most waste in the overall production process – in excess of 70% – happens before the end users gets their hands on materials or products. Production is very often subtractive, material is cut away to provide shape and form, and hence function. It's a 'heat, beat and treat' energy-intensive world too. What if production was additive, and materials were designed to 'fit' a circular economy?

"What is Direct Digital Manufacturing (DDM)?

DDM is the fabrication of components in a seamless manner from computer design to actual part in hand. Also know as '3D printing' or 'additive,' 'rapid,' 'instant,' 'on-demand' manufacturing, DDM uses 3D computer-aided design files to drive the computer-controlled fabrication of parts. Unlike traditional machining methods, which involve working from a rough mold and then cutting away to achieve the desired complex shape, direct digital manufacturing creates the shape precisely and instantly, using additive fabrication. DDM is commonly explained through the example of creating a coffee cup. An old-style craftsman might slowly shape a piece of clay by hand into a handmade mug. Designers and machinists in a factory would build a series of metallic molds and then create a series of tools to mill metal into the key components of the cup (handle, bottom, etc.), which would then be assembled on a production line, often through welding. By contrast, a DDM designer would create a digital 3D model of the cup, then turn production over to the computer, which would digitally slice it into a stack of wafer-thin layers, print them out, and fuse them together."

http://www.brookings.edu/research/articles/2011/10/
10-digital-manufacturing-singer

According to Mark Boyer, DDM is one of today's most exciting emerging technologies – few other developments have as much potential to shape the way we make things and the world as we know it. DDM is additive manufacturing, building up objects towards their final form and function

Closed sunflower

Photo: Shutterstock

rather than subtractive manufacturing so it has the immediate potential for being less wasteful, especially if the materials it builds from are carefully designed and chosen.

Just examining a catalogue for machine tools shows how much effort we currently put into the subtractive process. There is the energy required too. Manufacturing as 'heat, beat and treat' is crude and wasteful and the investment in large plants to benefit from economies of scale in this exercise also means shipping and other distribution costs. How much more elegant for the designs to criss-cross the globe digitally than the objects or the materials. Materials are key. Currently the choice of DDM materials is far from being local, abundant, safe or digestible: 3D printers are using the same old fossil fuel-based polymers and resins that end up in landfill or incinerators. Although the technology is young and materials will become more sophisticated and varied Janine Benyus cautions against such an assumption. Janine is most famous for her book *Biomimicry*[2] and the establishment of Biomimicry 3.8, a hub for developing the understanding of what insights from living systems – rather than Nature as a resource – can teach us. She has a very different message: we need a DDM revolution developing printing processes modeled on the way nature builds living organisms.

Mark Boyer[3] takes up the story in a report for Inhabitat from a Global Biomimicry Conference held in June 2013:

"...complex materials can be simplified, Benyus argues, and the key to making 3D printing more sustainable can be found in the natural systems all around us. Nature relies on a very small set of 'feedstocks,' or raw materials; a set of just five polymers make up most biomaterials found in nature, and 3D printing should adopt a similar five-polymer system so that materials can be fed back into a printer for reuse when they are no longer needed.

As an example of the divide that exists between complex manmade objects and simple materials found in nature, Benyus compares a beetle's shell with a bag of potato chips. Both serve several crucial functions; the beetle's shell provides strength, breathability and waterproofing, while the chip bag is waterproof, airtight, and has labels printed on it. But in contrast to the shell, which is made of only one polymer – chitin – the chip bag contains different materials for each function. After the beetle dies, the shell biodegrades, but the chip bag is difficult to recycle.

Photo: Thinkstock

In order to be more like the beetle shell and less like the chip bag, Benyus argues that 3D printing must conform to three basic principles:

1. The materials must be made from a small set of locally sourced, non-toxic and recyclable polymer feedstocks.

2. The structural designs used in 3D printing must mimic those found in nature, imparting strength and flexibility.

3. A 'take-back' system must be instituted that will enable products to be reconfigured as feedstock.

One of the most exciting things about 3D printing is that it has the potential to put the means of production in the hands of consumers. But that can only be realized if the materials used are greatly simplified so that source materials are, in Benyus' words, "common, abundant, and local". In addition to democratizing the manufacture of products, 3D printing has the potential to blossom into a truly innovative ... system by mimicking the circular flow of materials in the natural world."

In the inner circles of the technical cycle in a circular economy, instead of recycling materials, the challenge is around creating easier pathways to extending use – repair, refurbishment etc – and upgrading and generally increasing access (more use of the asset in a particular time period). Just as the (ongoing) digital revolution has created the means to track stuff, and monitor the functioning of appliances and charge per use, DDM has also begun to have an impact on how and when and where and for what purpose manufacturing is undertaken. DDM feels heaven-sent for a circular economy which is in need of regional or local access to achieve repair and refurbishment of smaller flows of more intensively used assets over longer periods – whether machines or buildings or apple orchards. It is important to recognise that DDM is not the same as returning 'back to the 1950s' approach when motorbikes or household appliances, for example, might have lasted a long time (in theory) but were unsophisticated, needed regular routine maintenance, and were inefficient in energy and materials and often very expensive – and importantly, unavailable to the majority.

Vincent Comet Motorbike 1952. It cost the equivalent of 2.5 years' wages for the average worker. No average worker could expect to own one.

Photo: www.motorcycles20thcentury.com/Bert Knoester

Disruptive Manufacturing according to *The Economist*

"Everything in the factories of the future will be run by smarter software. Digitisation in manufacturing will have a disruptive effect every bit as big as in other industries that have gone digital, such as office equipment, telecoms, photography, music, publishing and films. And the effects will not be confined to large manufacturers; indeed, they will need to watch out because much of what is coming will empower small and medium-sized firms and individual entrepreneurs. Launching novel products will become easier and cheaper. Communities offering 3D printing and other production services that are a bit like Facebook are already forming online – a new phenomenon which might be called social manufacturing.

The consequences of all these changes amount to a third industrial revolution. The first began in Britain in the late 18th century with the mechanisation of the textile industry. In the following decades the use of machines to make things, instead of crafting them by hand, spread around the world. The second industrial revolution began in America in the early 20th century with the assembly line, which ushered in the era of mass production.

As manufacturing goes digital, a third great change is now gathering pace. It will allow things to be made economically in much smaller numbers, more flexibly and with a much lower input of labour, thanks to new materials, completely new processes such as 3D printing, easy-to-use robots and new collaborative manufacturing services available online. The wheel is almost coming full circle, turning away from mass manufacturing and towards much more individualised production. And that in turn could bring some of the jobs back to rich countries that long ago lost them to the emerging world."

© *The Economist* Newspaper Limited, London 2012

It is a triangular, reinforcing arrangement:
• the circular economy of well-designed products designed for the full cycle and disassembly using 'clean' materials (with a shift towards renewables and needing energy lower thresholds as a result);
• meets a sharing economy which is independently about finding access to assets rather than ownership fired up by information technology advances;
• meets digital manufacturing with its 3D printers, rapid prototyping and customisation, its laser cutters and precise CNC (Computer Numerical Control) routers.

Plus a happy ethos of shared working amongst artisans – in the MakerLabs or FabLab style! Additionally, attention might shift to DDM processes, which are often less wasteful than subtractive manufacturing and excitingly allow us potential access to the lessons living systems provide where the use of structure is much more important and the palette of materials is more restrictive.

Here is the key to that repair and refurbish and repurposing possibility which had all but disappeared in the era of global supply chains based on mass production and the 'easier to buy a new one than fix it' approach. Scatter a pocketful of instructional YouTube videos on iFixit[4] e.g. on how to make a new ceramic part for your Panasonic breadmaker or the latest modification to get around a design flaw in a petrol garden strimmer or post on Facebook or Twitter about the next pop-up repair café in your town. Then garnish with the global eBay network which means you can buy what you are missing for even the most obscure item. No wonder car boot sales are a treasure trove these days. Add in the open-source design movement and crowd-funding innovations which can back the outsider to win, and it becomes a very, very potent mix. It's an ideal scenario for the insurgents, the new businesses on the block looking for the cracks in the pavement and very challenging for the incumbents, the established businesses, if only because the situation is so fluid.

An example of a combination of these forces in action is the Global Village Construction Set (GVCS)[5] which comprises "an advanced industrial economy-in-a-box that can be replicated inexpensively anywhere in the world. The GVCS is like a Lego set of modular building blocks that work together – creating sustainable, regenerative, resilient communities."

It is striking how this project clearly has a 'big picture' sense of what it wants to achieve, using some of the best creative and collaborative tools to come out of the digital age. In its own words it "combines appropriate technology, high technology, resilient community development, sustainable living, economic development, automation, open source product development, community construction, open source economic development, and livelihood topics."

Perhaps it is the audacity of the whole thing and its clear references to radical designers like Buckminster Fuller which also appeals. As a retake on how to create abundance by "questioning everything you thought you knew about building communities", while adding a sense of fun and engagement, it is a fantastic talking point, truly educational.

Is this putative 'open source economy' part of a 'circular economy'? It could be argued that it looks more like a social enterprise providing people with tools – and the means for their use and maintenance – a sort of 'post oil' community building … but just a moment – a circular economy requires, absolutely requires, a way of restoring and rebuilding social and natural capital. It also requires us to rebuild economies in a way which gives people opportunities to work at a wide range of scales and meet more of their own needs. The GVCS machines are also claimed to be much cheaper than commercial tools and make much use of standardised components. It's affordable.

The sharing economy practitioners describe a shift from a job for life, to a series of careers, to several jobs at once, so it's very contemporary. It is still vitally important for waste to be food and there to be technical and biological cycles. The GVCS tools are designed to be fixable, repairable, reusable and they hardly consist of the sort of kit which would end up in landfill.

This is why the GVCS is such an interesting concept; it is creative and challenging. Circular economy, sharing economy/performance economy, digital manufacturing and perhaps, lastly, a devolved economy too. In these days when tools and ideas and energy are being decentralised to communities of many kinds and spread at digital speed, it is the institutions, most of which have a reluctance or inability to adapt, who may be most surprised by this innovation. These developments that spring up all over the place and find traction may simply bypass traditional structures.

THE GLOBAL VILLAGE CONSTRUCTION SET

Some key features include a proposed set of 50 cheap but modern tools providing people with technology to do more with less, open-source development so that a global community can contribute and share the development and the benefits, a wide range of interchangeable parts, and new approaches to familiar problems.

The tools include a microhouse, bulldozer, tractor, dairy milker, bakery oven and well-drilling rig through to a 3D scanner and 3D printer, power cube and plasma cutter.

The creators of the set, Open Source Ecology, freely publish their 3D designs, schematics, instructional videos, budgets, and product manuals on an open-source wiki. Users can produce and modify the tool set.

They claim that the cost of making or buying their machines is, on average, eight times cheaper than buying from an industrial manufacturer, including an average labor cost of USD 25 per hour for a GVCS fabricator. For example the tractor comes in at under USD 5,000 compared to USD 20,000 or more for one produced by an industrial brand, while a skid loader costs just a few hundred dollars rather than USD 20,000. As well as designing some parts to be interchangeable; tools are designed for disassembly enabling the user to take apart, maintain, and fix them readily.

FAB LAB MANCHESTER

The UK's first Fab Lab opened in Manchester in March 2010. It is owned by The Manufacturing Institute and managed by its staff. It is located in the Chips building in New Islington, Manchester.

At the heart of Fab Lab Manchester is digital manufacturing technology including laser and vinyl cutters, CNC routers, vacuum former and an embroidery machine. The Lab can produce a single unique product from a digital design in a matter of minutes and at a very low cost in comparison to traditional tooling methods.

To date, 3,000 small manufacturers, inventors, schools and community groups have used Fab Lab Manchester with a wide range of products having been conceived, developed and prototyped there.

Finally, Jocelyn Blériot on the rise of urban mining...

Trapped between high hopes placed on the potential of materials that have yet to be invented and the growing concern generated by the need to mine more stuff, we often seem to overlook the wealth of resources already in circulation. Yet the heritage of the industrial era is such that mature markets are a world where a considerable amount of the extraction/production work has already been done.

And if the ambition is to create an economy based on effective, carefully managed and pure material flows, then including these 'overground resources' in the master plan is fundamental: the current economic context confirms, on a daily basis, that what fuelled prosperity until the dawn of the 21st century cannot be relied upon anymore. So, rather than focus on reductionist tactics, we should start considering making better use of the existing assets. As Thomas E. Graedel (Yale School of Forestry and Environmental Science) puts it:

"A half century ago, the visionary urbanist Jane Jacobs (1961) proclaimed that

' Cities are the mines of the future. '

This prediction was based on some hard facts that are more evident today than they were when Jacobs penned her words."[6]

What Professor Graedel refers to when he talks about urban mining naturally goes way beyond what the expression evokes on a superficial level – images of disorganised scavenging may spring to mind. Yet the reality of the concept as it stands today involves careful stock assessment, periodic tables and timelines recapitulating materials availability.

Jesse Stallone, co-founder of urbanmining.org, describes this idea as "the process of reclaiming compounds and elements from products, building and waste (...) [It goes] beyond 'Dumpster Diving', [and] requires a systems approach that utilises industrial ecology when viewing our end-of-pipe activities for material recovery." The expression is often used to describe the recovery process of precious metals from old electronic devices, and with roughly 30 times more gold in mobile phone circuitry than in ore as processed in mines on a tonne to tonne basis, the potential seems striking.[7] But urban mining is not limited to delicate retrieval operations to salvage metals that are sought-after by jewellers. It also applies to large-scale materials pools we too often neglect.

As Professor Graedel explains:

"The energy used for primary production is embodied, to a large extent, in the metal and, consequently, in the building too. Today's buildings and their contents therefore present large 'urban mines' of around 400 million tonnes of aluminium metal[8] that can be extracted and recycled by future generations through the use of only 5% of the originally used energy, not just once but repeatedly."

To deliberately simplify things, imagine a young boy in his playroom, his mind set on building a new house with Lego bricks, because his previous creation – still standing – does not satisfy the needs of the new generation of Lego people that just arrived in the region. To his left stands the previous dwelling, disused but made of carefully selected bricks, to his right a boxful of muddled-up individual components (let's consider that the selection process represents, by analogy, the raw materials transformation which happens in the 'real world'). Where would you, in his place, source your materials from? Time and energy are the most two obvious savings to be within reach in this analogy, and in a real-world scenario one would need to add on top of those a financial gain and a reduction of negative impacts (due to mining and production, and transport).

Depending on their scarcity level, ease of recovery, ability to be reprocessed etc., materials have to be plotted into a 'periodic table of recyclability' and classified according to the nature of their stock. Graedel makes a clear distinction between 'abandoned' (i.e. very hard or impossible to recover), 'comatose' (recovery is unlikely) and 'hibernating' (currently not performing a useful service) stocks. For certain metals, such as copper, the fact that a potential 95% saving in terms of energy can be achieved opens up the discussion on to new horizons from a systems perspective. Placing that energy factor in the wider debate about changing our linear model actually addresses some of the issues usually raised when it comes to moving towards renewable energy: urban mining rolled out at scale could potentially play an important role in achieving threshold efficiency.

Technologies and economics often combine in new and unexpected ways and it is perhaps no surprise to see additive manufacture, relocalisation of production and recovery of materials all being a part of a different energy demand and supply mix. The barriers to change are mostly in our head. Seeing renewables as a swap out for big-box one-way fossil fuel energy systems based on throughput linear economies is naïve. It was never going to happen. But as part of a much smarter industrial system, with effective extended product life, good design, effective materials recovery and the possibilities of sharing and collaborative consumption, it looks very different.

PLASTIC AND STONE PAPER

The first edition of Bill McDonough's and Michael Braungart's book *Cradle to Cradle* was printed on Mechcher Media DuraBooks synthetic paper made from inorganic fillers and plastic resins. The DuraBook is a technical nutrient or material i.e. it can be processed back into the raw material for a new book more rapidly and at lower cost – in terms of energy and materials as well as the level of toxicity engendered by many recycled paper de-inking processes. Yes, it costs more, almost anything done on a limited scale compared to a very large scale can be financially more expensive. But as Pauli has noted,[9] just focussing on the one valuable element rather than the potential from multiple cashflows or perhaps other positive consequences can often be accompanied by the sound and effect of unmet costs being ladled overboard from the business: the 'externalities' problem.

The point being made about the book as a material is that the plastic once in a plastic cycle can stay there – if the materials system to deal with these books is in place of course. A BIG 'if'. It's the scale question in part. Just like a biodegradable plastic bottle appearing in the massive PET plant, the plastic book is a contaminant – something the system cannot deal with easily. But sufficient 'contaminant' objects warrants a process to filter them out; and an avalanche of them demands a new business. A diversity of routes through to material recovery could be envisaged, but again a narrow definition of efficiency supported by financial incentives around displacing labour and using more capital and energy makes this more nuanced approach more difficult. To work it requires a good material in an amenable materials system but one that also makes sense economically.

ANTI-MOTH   TEAR RESISTANT   PHOTO-DEGRADABLE   RECYCLABLE

SAFE   SOFT   WATER RESISTANT   ECONOMICAL

Some characteristics of stone paper. Cradle to cradle certified stone paper made by Taiwan Lung Meng Technology Co.

This brings us to stone paper... about 80% rock and 20% plastic and pretty much recyclable for ever.

All rock waste can be converted to stone paper, here is Pauli's riff on the possibilities:

"Producing paper from pulverized rocks offers an opportunity to produce tree-free paper, manufactured without any water and is 100% recyclable forever. This means that over time the vast swathes of land reserved for forests could be substituted by a permanent stock of paper. The cost is now converted into an asset, very much like aluminum cans have ended up on balance sheets instead of mere costs of packaging. The substitution of pulp with stone (and a small percentage of recycled plastics) will free up millions of hectares of land and puts our drive towards food security in another dimension. Mining that supports agriculture seems far fetched indeed, but is a reality once we consider the whole system."

This discussion is important, quite apart from whether stone paper could release land for other purposes. It is a reminder that communities are driven by adding value, not by having cheaper products. Mining and agriculture look quaint in economies dominated by services and eventually financial services – the latter mainly in the digital realm. But if the mining and agriculture sectors fail to provide a means of adding value for communities, then additional efficiencies, leading to labour displacement, will only serve up more jobless growth and increased demand for, and dependency on, government support to the very poorest – paid for by taxes and deficit spending. A means of adding value which could well mean a revival of both primary and secondary production is not at all far-fetched.

Photo: Jocelyn Bériot

9 THE REGENERATIVE BIOLOGICAL CYCLE - AT SCALE

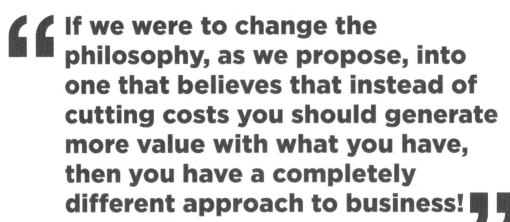

If we were to change the philosophy, as we propose, into one that believes that instead of cutting costs you should generate more value with what you have, then you have a completely different approach to business!

Gunter Pauli

There is much flag waving for the idea of an 'upcycle', a positive cycle where a circular economy is not just enduring but restorative or regenerative. More a spiral than a circle of course. Needless to say, this is a tough call in a world of take, make and dispose where food from South Africa is consumed in Russia or where 70% of the world's production of children's toys takes place in China but their use clearly does not. Any naïve idea of 'loop closing' on this sort of geographical scale is not going to happen, except as downcycling perhaps. The restorative and regenerative notion is energising, however: to rebuild natural (and social) capital in order to produce more and better goods and services and in the longer term. In Chapter 5 attention shifted to what can be achieved by better understanding stocks and flows.

Application of technology and products has generated impressive results over the last 50 years

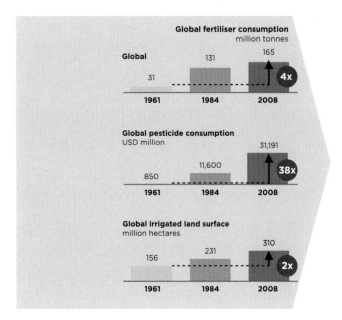

Rapidly growing supply

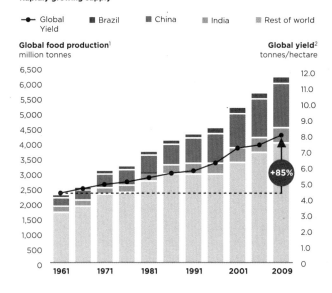

1 Includes cereals, citrus fruit, course grain, primary fibre crops, fruit, primary oil crops, pulses, roots and tubers, tree nuts, vegetables

2 Weighted average of the above agricultural products

Source: FAO; Zhang, Jiang and Ou, 2011

This chapter goes in search of some of the keys to large-scale examples of how a restorative economy might be observed and developed. It finds them in the semi-arid grasslands, in the tropical food crop areas and in the rice paddies. The key was knowledge, but a systems perspective kind of knowledge, and one which had to be established – or better, rediscovered and fought for – against a backdrop of inertia, conventional wisdom and failure.

In the idealised schematic of a circular economy (page 19) the loop is eventually closed on the biological side and on land via the agency of sunlight, fungi and bacteria and the other communities of life in the soil. Here, then, soil is a simplified notion of natural capital in agricultural systems. As in the case of technical materials flows, it is easy to demonstrate the extractive and capital-reducing qualities of the existing linear system which has successfully substituted fossil fuel derived fertilisers, new crop and livestock configurations and machinery for labour in return for increased thoughput.[1] See graphs on previous page.

"Today's agriculture does not allow the soil to enrich itself, but depends on chemical fertilisers that don't replace the wide variety of nutrients plants and humans need" says Dr Tim Lobstein, the UK's Food Commission director. Land degradation costs an estimated USD 40 billion annually worldwide, without taking into account the costs of increased fertiliser use, loss of biodiversity, and loss of unique landscapes.[2]

Soil degradation is estimated to extend to some 25–35% of the 1.5 billion hectares of land under cultivation, meaning that it is less fertile, less able to retain water, less able to fend off pests, and more prone to erosion. Loss of soil carbon is problematic given the role of this carbon in several developing and maintaining factors that are critical to plant growth, such as soil texture, water retention and nutrient delivery to the roots of plants. In Europe, around 45% of soils have low or very low organic matter content, 45% have medium content.[3]

The maps overleaf remind us of the extent and importance of agriculture as it relates to human welfare across large swathes of the world: in the savannah grasslands (cattle), sugar cane growing (crop monocultures) and paddy rice areas.

Between these three modes of agriculture it is possible to capture an excellent spread around some of the challenges of falling carbon content, deteriorating soil structure, desertification and excessive use of artificial fertiliser and pesticides and their 'downstream' externalities.

Gunter Pauli, in a 2013 interview with consultancy EMG describes how his innovation in the use of palm oil as a detergent base didn't work as expected: "I created the Ecover factory around 20 years ago, and all that time it has relied on palm oil to create many of its products; the same palm oil that is continuing to destroy rainforests. So I have to look at myself and consider the mistakes that I have made. In those days, I did not see that I was destroying the rainforest. But now I know!"

His failure was in a lack of systems thinking. In this example, the Ecover detergent helped to improve the quality of water in European rivers but led to accelerated rainforest destruction in Indonesia. After the experience, the learning.

It was a similar experience for Alan Savory who now heads research into holistic cattle grazing systems at the Savory Institute, USA. He was once responsible for the decision in what was Rhodesia (Zimbabwe) to cull thousands of African elephants in the belief that reduced grazing would slow down or reverse the decline in the savannah grasslands. He bitterly regrets this decision and admits that he was completely wrong. He had failed to understand the system, the way these grasslands had evolved and the place of grazing, plant-eating animals.

The conventional wisdom is that reduced grazing is better – it sounds right. More herbivores, such as elephants or cattle, means more stress on the vegetation and less output and falling soil quality. But this is a partial understanding. Alan Savory came to realize that, in evolutionary terms, the grasslands developed in the presence of very large herds of herbivores and that this characteristic – of a large herd grazing everything, churning up the soil with their hooves and depositing faeces and urine and slobber before moving on – had a particular relevance to how the grassland worked as a system.

Taking it to the other extreme, Savory found evidence that leaving a semi-arid grassland without cattle or other herbivores means it doesn't thrive, it becomes 'stagnant' – sub-optimal but reasonably stable. Nutrients are not returning to the soil as they are locked up in the dead stalks and stems of the earlier years, since rainfall is low and bacteria and fungi cannot get to work as they would prefer. Moreover sun-baked, bare earth develops a crust so that rain runs off more easily, land erodes and water which runs off is not available for plants – and brings flooding downstream. Some woody perennial plants begin to dominate and species diversity in the system declines.

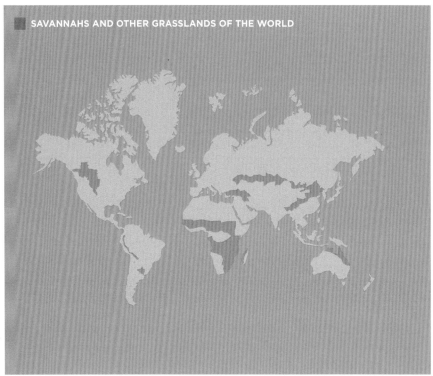

SAVANNAHS AND OTHER GRASSLANDS OF THE WORLD

Source: NASA   Indicative only

In savannah that is intensely grazed by herds which then move on, the situation is very different. The stomachs of the cattle act as bioreactors. The water needed by bacteria and the bacteria themselves are active in the cattle stomachs and the resulting manures and urine are rich in minerals. In addition, the cattle hooves break up the soil surface and the non-discriminatory grazing leaves spaces for plants which would lose out in the ungrazed regime – particularly annual grasses.

It is the way the grasses react which is most interesting. Once heavily grazed, the grasses adapt their root structure to the needs of regrowth, effectively 'dropping' some roots since the structure above ground is much reduced: as the plant grows again the roots will regrow. This process 'pulses' carbon into the soils, but the key is that the new plant growth isn't grazed too soon. That herd needs to be long gone and for quite a while. In conventional cattle grazing the interval between grazing periods is too short and the pressure on the habitat limits diverse plant species regrowth – the animals are choosy eaters if they can be and the energy of the grasses is never fully rebuilt.

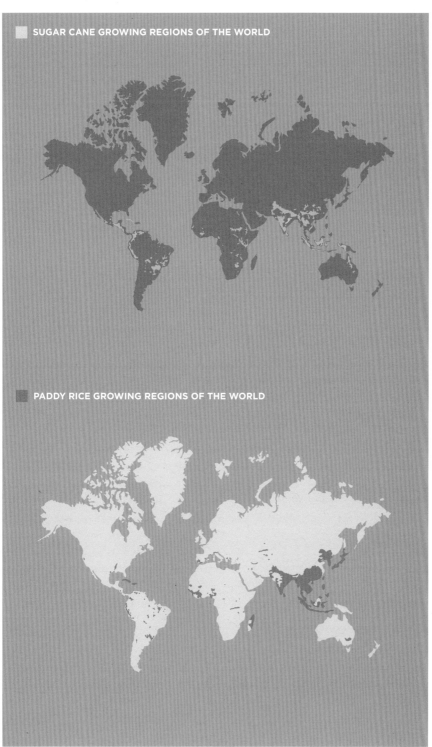

SUGAR CANE GROWING REGIONS OF THE WORLD

PADDY RICE GROWING REGIONS OF THE WORLD

Source: NASA

Indicative only

The two diagrams below show how Savory believes the cycle of carbon loss from conventional and what he terms holistic grazing can be illustrated. In the holistic system at Savory Institute cattle grazing is established to mimic the grazing patterns of herbivores in natural savannah ecosystems – this ensures more effective nutrient cycling and build up of soil organic matter resulting in enhanced vegetation growth and cattle grazing land.

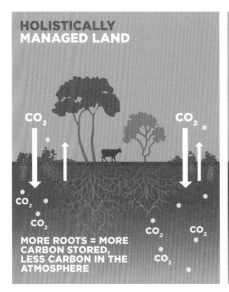
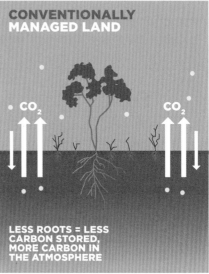

The photo opposite of cattle grazing lush ranchland[4] gives some clue to what a restorative biological cycle means: in this case better water retention as carbon levels are built up in vegetation and soil systems, leading to more resilience during drought periods; better output in terms of cattle per hectare; less soil erosion and greater biodiversity. Better flood control is a by-product for land downstream. All these benefits really need to be accounted for, but most are not. If a shallower focus is allowed, the plus is just more cattle. It sounds rather mean-spirited.

There are plenty of critics when it comes to such systems adjustment approaches, not least in that identifying what matters and what does not in a complex system is always up for debate. Often the objections run deeper. It is just not how we do things – focussing down on core competencies, defined outcomes feels like work and being in charge, whereas looking up to system level and waiting on the return of a certain fungus feels 'woolly' or imprecise. Which of course it is, these being complex adaptive systems with histories! The choice here of the work of the Savory Institute was made not least because something positive is happening as far as its practitioners are concerned and at scale. It is the same with the following case study, from the world of monocultures.

Cattle ranch in Oregon, USA. Organic grass-fed beef cattle feeding on native grassland species
Photo: Keystone USA-ZUMA/Rex

CASE STUDY 1

Leontino Balbo supplies over a third of all organic sugar on the world market. His aim is to obtain great returns in terms of output but by restoring the quality of the soil. This from an interview in *Wired* **Magazine:**

"Soil is not just a container," he says, "it's also the content of the ecosystem. It holds the biodiversity, both living and mineral, that's essential for life. If the soil loses this function, all other things are compromised." According to Balbo, modern agriculture damages soil in three ways. Farm machinery compresses it, making it less able to hold water; fertilisers upset its natural chemical balance; and monocrops reduce its biodiversity, which he sees as essential for healthy plants. "So much soil used for agriculture is dead... we need to revitalise it, to restore the energy of its ecosystem," he says.

Perhaps the most remarkable characteristic of his work over nearly 30 years is just that: how long it took to solve some of the puzzle – and it's not over yet.

"All along it has been like I have been doing a 10,000-piece jigsaw puzzle and now I have about 100 pieces to go. We will be able to produce cane sugar at half the cost of conventional production today, providing all those environmental benefits and using a third of the resources. That's what makes me so enthusiastic."[5]

It was fortunate that Balbo was the heir to the family sugar plantations and could experiment with large blocks of cropland. In his story he emphasises not only that conventional scientific analyses were not helpful, and were indeed discouraging to his efforts for the most part, but the breadth of knowledge and skills he had to master in order to make sense of both the challenge and the solutions. His ambitions sound very big picture and also centre around knowledge transfer. His system he calls ecosystem revitalizing agriculture or ERA.

" My first and main concern is to offer an alternative production model to chemical systems. I intend to charge growers a certain amount per hectare of land where the technology is applied, and find a way they can pay me back from the additional revenues that ERA will provide. It is not my goal, like some big corporations do, to make the growers dependent on the system or to add extra costs. This technology aims to make the growers independent again, after almost four decades of domination (by big business). "

Balbo's family business is doing well, producing 75,000 tonnes of organic sugar – 34% of the world market and a figure he is planning to raise as demand increases – and 55,000m³ of organic ethanol each year from a crop of about 1.2 million tonnes of cane. His sugar is used in about 120 high-profile products from Green & Black's chocolate to Yeo Valley yoghurt. On the farm, energy use has fallen by half and, when the introduction of green-cane harvesting threatened the jobs of the manual labourers who had previously cut the crop, he ensured that they were retrained and found work elsewhere on the plantation. All Balbo employees now have access to welfare, medical and sports facilities, and low-cost housing.

Ricardo Abramovay, professor of economics at the University of São Paulo, who researches large-scale agriculture: "He has achieved what many consider impossible; a large continuous area occupied by a single product that still provides exceptionally favourable conditions not only for agriculture but also for wildlife."

Leotino Balbo Junior inspects his sugar cane fields

Photo: Matthew Mahon/Redux

CASE STUDY 2

The last example is from the paddy rice fields. Once more the challenge is in understanding the inter-relationships in the system to create multiple benefits, multiple cash flows and a positive cycle. Perhaps it is the other way around. Understand the positive cycle and see what can be harvested from it. Build the capital and then draw down the appropriate income.

Takao Furono is a farmer from southern Japan who has experimented extensively with the design and development of duck/rice/fish farming systems. Rather than grow rice as a monoculture crop, that depends on fossil fuel fertilisers and pesticides to achieve high crop yields, Furono has developed a complex, species-rich system that has increased his farm's rice yields whilst producing a wide range of other food products – without depending on any outside crop inputs.

Photo: Imagine China/Rex

Frederick Kirschenmann from Iowa State University has studied how this particular farm system works:

ff ...after Mr Furono sets his rice seedlings out into his flooded rice paddies, he puts a gaggle of young ducklings into the paddies. The ducklings immediately start to feed on insects that normally attack young rice plants. Mr Furono then introduces loaches, a variety of fish that is easily cultivated and produces a delicious meat product. He also introduces azolla, normally considered a 'paddy weed'. The azolla fixes nitrogen but also serves as food for the fish and the ducks. In this way Mr Furono has developed a highly synergistic farming system. The ducks feed on the insects and, later, the golden snails that attack rice plants. Since the ducks and fish feed on the azolla, its growth is kept sufficiently under control so it does not compete with the growing rice, but serves as a source of nitrogen. The nitrogen from the azolla, plus the droppings from the ducks and fish, provides all the nutrients needed for the rice. 》》 [6]

The ducks also eat the seeds and seedlings of weeds, using their feet to dig up the weed seedlings, thus oxygenating the water and encouraging the roots of the rice plants to grow. The ducks are so effective at weeding that farmers who have adopted this farming system avoid an estimated 240 person hours per hectare in manual weeding every year.[7] The ducks are completely free ranging on the farm until the rice plants form ears of grain in the field. At that stage, the ducks have to be rounded up otherwise they will eat the rice grains. They are then confined in a shed and fed exclusively on waste rice grain.

In addition, Furono grows figs on the edges of his rice paddy fields, supplying him with fruit. He then rotates his integrated rice/duck crop with a crop of vegetables and wheat so as to prevent the buildup of pests in the farm soil. He also harvests duck eggs that he markets along with the rice, fish and duck meat, vegetables, wheat and figs. His cash flows from the farm are also enhanced by the fact that his rice yields in this system exceed the rice yields of industrial rice systems by 20-50%.[8] This farm design modelled on complex dynamic living systems makes Furono's farm in Japan extremely productive in international terms. According to conversations he has had with modern monoculture rice growers in Texas, the gross income from Furono's 6-acre farm in Japan slightly exceeds the gross income of a typical 600-acre rice farm in Texas.

Takao Furono has successfully marketed his rice which now sells at a 20-30% premium over conventionally grown rice in Japan and other countries. Today, his small farm gives him an income of USD160,000 a year from producing rice, organic vegetables and fruit, eggs and ducklings. After demonstrating small-scale organic farming systems can be highly productive, he is disseminating his ideas. A film of his work has been produced[9] and through writing, lectures and cooperation with agricultural organisations and governments, his methods have spread to more than 75,000 small-scale farmers in Japan as well as South Korea, Vietnam, the Philippines, Laos, Cambodia, Malaysia, China, Taiwan, India, Cuba and Bangladesh.

This example is quite well established in the literature but the question might arise as to why, if it works, it is still a niche activity? While cheap(ish) fertilisers and simplified systems predominate (they have a comparatively low knowledge threshold), while costs are externalised and perhaps also while subsidiary markets for the other products of the duck–rice system are underdeveloped, the answer obvious is 'why bother?' As Frederick Kirschenmann points out, these highly productive, redesigned farming systems that mimic complex dynamic living ecosystems (in this case tropical freshwater wetland ecosystems) are most compatible with smaller scale, independently owned farms. Such complex systems do not seem to lend themselves well to large-scale centralised operations where farmers are not usually involved with the complex ecology of their farms.

Paradoxically the political call in these times is for a knowledge economy to meet demands for jobs and better incomes. Understanding the potential for adding value by understanding complex and dynamic systems with an upcycle potential seems to be a no brainer for jobs and income. Yet the education, or rather schooling, system is set in quite another direction, one entrained by the understanding that the world was a machine-like affair and knowledge means specialism and more knowledge, even more of it.

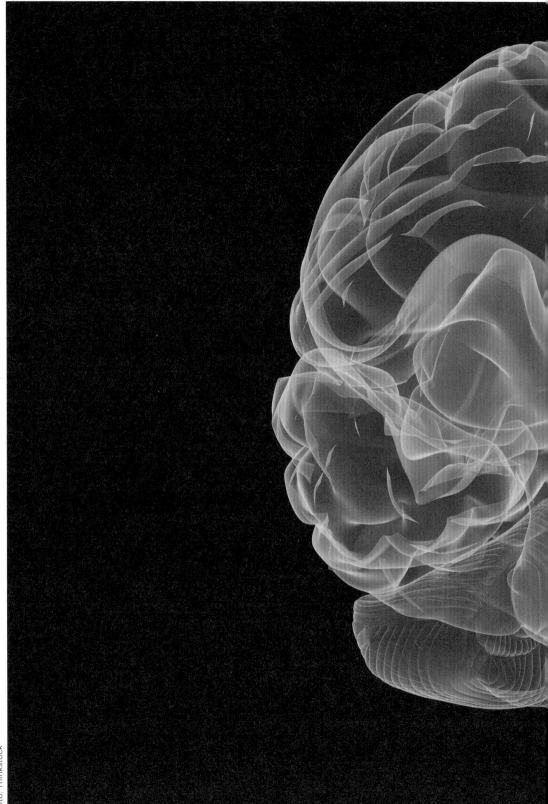

Photo: Thinkstock

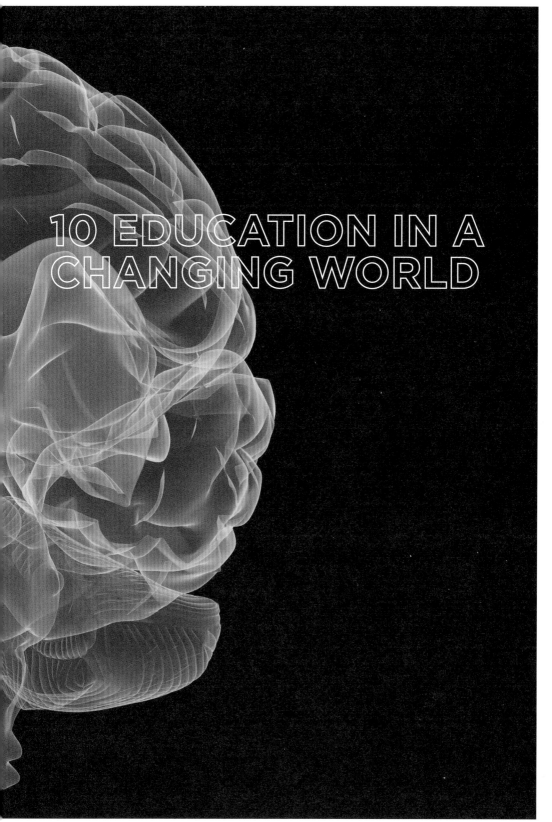

10 EDUCATION IN A CHANGING WORLD

We have to go from what is essentially an industrial model of education, a manufacturing model, which is based on linearity and conformity and batching people. We have to move to a model that is based more on principles of agriculture. We have to recognize that human flourishing is not a mechanical process; it's an organic process. And you cannot predict the outcome of human development. All you can do, like a farmer, is create the conditions under which they will begin to flourish.

Ken Robinson

Sir Ken Robinson is not the first person to point out the parallels between schooling as we know it and the linear industrial production lines which so characterised the traditional manufacturing plants of the 19th century and afterwards. Nor is he alone in using the metaphor of gardening to illustrate his version of "setting the system conditions and allowing iteration": Nick Hanauer and Eric Liu write of the 'Gardens of Democracy' in exactly the same way. But, mainstream it is not. We are in thrall to the past.

It comes as a surprise to many, however, to realise that the conformity, the standardisation, the isolation from the wider community, the examination of a narrow set of knowledge and skills was intended to mould pupils and students for just that sort of 19th-century urbanising factory-dominated economy. It was schooling, not education, since schooling accepts the ends as given while education does not.

A broader, more stimulating, open-ended curriculum was reserved for the universities and the elites who were assumed to enter them. The sop was that in a growing economy many more able young people would be needed and that social progress or elevation through meritocratic success was possible. The pay off was 'Jam tomorrow' for the hard working, but in any event 'employment for all' – despite schools' often uneven quality – was the prospect for the rest. This preparation for, variously, leadership, citizenship and for the marketplace was rooted in the nation-building intentions of Germany in the mid-19th century – it was described as the Prussian system – and spread widely from there.

We got the kind of schooling that reinforced the dominant economic ideas of the time. We got the kind of economic ideas that reflected the dominant scientific ideas of the time. We still do, or perhaps it is better to say that we always did. Except that the rate of change has been so great in both our scientific understanding and in the economy that schooling has suffered major dislocation. Since the 1980s, 'employment for all' has an increasingly hollow ring to it in the developed world, since the factories have gone abroad or are inhabited by robots and computers, and the part-time and service jobs which are available seem to barely require much schooling, let alone upwards of 12 years of it.

The expansion of university, or more broadly tertiary, education was supposed to be a response, to emphasise the role of a burgeoning knowledge and skills economy, coupled to the new job opportunities created by whole new industries spawned by technological change and increasing productivity. This would take up the slack. It did for a time, but two trends are evident now. On the one hand increasing numbers of graduates means increasing competition for the falling percentage of full-time permanent jobs in the professions and business, which reflects the falling number of permanent jobs in the economy as a whole. It has lowered the rewards and has driven up the barriers to entry: what once required a degree now requires a further degree, and, some would add, a suitable internship and an introduction. On the other hand the rising costs of extended study and the shift away from free education, in the Anglo-Saxon world at least, has reduced the monetary advantage of graduate employment. Indeed, a recent UK report suggested that 40% of graduates in the UK were not even in jobs which required a graduate.[1]

Paradoxically, in an era in which so much information, most knowledge and even a little wisdom is available at no or low cost across the connected globe, never has the cost of a suitable accreditation from

COLLEGE COSTS AND MEDIAN FAMILY INCOME, 1982–2012

Inflation-adjusted increases

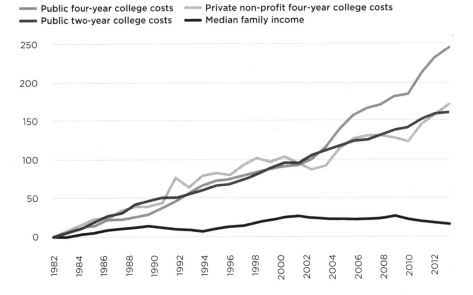

Sources: The College Board, Annual Survey of Colleges; National Centre for Educational Statistics, Integrated Post-secondary Education and Data System. Center for American Progress.

a leading university been so much, or rising so quickly. This highlights the often-heard contention that the schooling/education system is not primarily about learning, but about positioning for resources, access to the institutions, the centres of power and influence. The graph opposite highlights how rising education costs outstrip other costs in the USA, where there is upward of USD 1 trillion of student debt in play.[2] Higher education may be just the latest in a number of asset bubbles but it does not make it any the less real for those involved, or any the less puzzling when the mismatch is scrutinised between what is required for transition to a circular economy and what is available.

The challenge for schooling/training and education is at many levels all at the same time. At the top level we know that the real world is full of non-linear dynamic systems, of which the economy is only one, but one that is embedded in flows of energy, materials and information. This is the scientific challenge: to discuss these resource issues with the tools of today and tomorrow rather than those of yesterday and the 19th century. An associated challenge is that schools, for example, hardly teach any economics at all and where they do, it is largely the formalism of the world as equilibrium-seeking mechanism. At university level it is notorious that of nine economic schools of thought outlined by Cambridge University don Ha Joon Chang, in his book *Economics: A User's Guide*, only one – neo-classical economics – dominates university departments, to the extent that worldwide there have been protests and student boycotts against this extraordinary lack of pluralism. If the state of, and prospects for the economy are of central concern to young people (to everyone!) then it seems odd that it is not a concern of schooling in general. And similarly, at university level it is strange that only one (neo-classical) story is taught; particularly when we reflect on the role of universities and institutions in reproducing ideas which are used politically.

This is not a hopeless situation but the siloing of schooling along traditional subject boundaries undermines the attempts at making a systems perspective, which includes economics, the dominant approach, not a special case for occasional consideration. The circular economy becomes a minor part of something minor right from the get go. This will not assist its rapid uptake.

Buckminster Fuller noted that

"A designer is an emerging synthesis of artist, inventor, mechanic, objective economist and evolutionary strategist."

So where will these kinds of people come from? As now, perhaps, from the eccentrics and misfits and those too young to be intimidated, but reserving for these people some sort of against-the-odds-hero status is perverse in the extreme.

Further down the hierarchy, looking at the individual school or college, examining resources and choices in the widest sense, could the circular economy be taking its place or perhaps be changing what is understood in geography, in sustainability, biology, design technology or some more general sense of problem solving or skills development? There is a good reservoir of teachers and many enthusiastic learners who wish to see change for the better, a more prosperous, thriving world and citizens active in their democracies. This has been true for decades but there is no evidence that it has operated to create more than in a piecemeal fashion. A further challenge is the 'how to' of the style of teaching and learning which would be consistent with understanding aspects of a circular economy. Outside a case for integrating some case studies and details of new business models in business education, the circular economy represents a part of a changing mindset, not a bit of content. It's hard to escape the big picture demands of the circular economy in worldview, pedagogy, skills and aptitudes as well as new knowledge (see diagram on page 186 for the mutually reinforcing feedback around how we understand the world, learning and the economy).

The essence of the discussion in this book is how the systems conditions in the economy either reinforce a vicious cycle of accelerating throughput with all its downsides growing inexorably and outweighing the gains (or restricting them to small and shrinking sectors of the population), or how the conditions might reinforce a more virtuous cycle where significant advantages compound through time to more sectors as it becomes more complete. But where in the schooling context do we get a chance to compare different narratives about the economy, with their resonant and profound differences and consequences? Neither is all this a recent concern. Thomas Berry wrote in 1978:

"It's all a question of story. We are in trouble just now because we do not have a good story. We are in between stories. The Old Story is not functioning properly and we have not learned the New Story."[3]

A REFLECTION ON EDUCATION AND CHANGING MINDSETS

In the absence of very much in the way of economic literacy in schools the default mindset so often associated with phrases like 'resource constraints' or 'sustainable development', has been in practice a focus on just three things, the individual, consumption and guilt.

Schools deal with individuals: individuals being schooled to be good citizens. Individuals as key to the economy through their purchases and choices. Thus change is often treated primarily as a question of modifying individual behaviour and hoping that this in aggregate will 'make a difference'. Not changing behaviours is subject to a degree of self-imposed or institutionally sponsored 'guilt'. 'Oh dear, it's a mess and we created it.' Guilt, as we know, is singularly demotivating.

Some institutions have usefully made resource saving a feature of the campus generally. The 'debate' falls out then around individual behaviour and campus activities – changed light bulbs, new boilers and the like. Practical stuff. But in the realm of ideas, economics are dealt with very unsteadily. As an example, one idea often introduced to students is of reducing overall consumption in the richer nations, so as to take the pressure off pollution and waste, and/or to allow more resources for emerging economies. But there is no attendant discussion on the question, for example, about how this will work without bringing recession and lower living standards and how this would then leave the developing nations if we were not buying their products in the same quantity.

The suggestion to learners might also reasonably be made to consider life with less in a different and 'simpler' society: localised, low-energy, frugal with resources and closer to the land. It could almost appear to liberate the individual from the 'temptation and greed' built into our modern lifestyles – it could build social capital (interdependence) and substitute for those businesses that have been selling 'excess' and frippery. Austerity, by choice, as a means of atonement for our profligacy? It is really quite a romantic suggestion overlaid with morality. For some sections of society

– often it should be said, professionals, who love the idea of the craft bakery and the dignity of a decent day's 'hands on' work – this may sound attractive (if only in the mind or following a successful career in IT and after settling in an expensive rural village).

Could developing nations, for example, possibly 'save themselves' from crass modernity by taking this low-impact path now? In reality, a bicycle is less favoured than the moped and in turn the car and ... the discussion really lacks economics at that systems level. It feels as if discussion is boxed up.

The three columns of the below table represent different categories of thinking about the future. The question is 'which way out?' The top row of orange boxes offers three 'solutions' that might be reached without holding the linear or mechanistic worldview up for scrutiny. The bottom row offers options with a systems perspective. The earlier discussion about schools, for example, fits what is a moderation of the linear perspective by changed values or choosing a systems approach with a pre-industrial 'craft' bias (the centre column).

WHICH WAY OUT?

Mode	Little choice	Change values	Evolve the system
Linear	Do nothing, it's the order of things, let the poor make their own way. Defend what we have – a 'laager' mentality	Do with less. Reduce consumption and waste so that others can have a share. Green and ethical consumerism included	Economic growth and technological innovation will allow us to overcome the challenges
Systems	It's too late to do much but cope with a changed planet. Climate change, end of fossil fuel era. A lifeboat option	Go back. Adopt insights from pre-industrial era and emphasise self-reliance, local and shared 'loops'	**?**

What goes in the last box? A systems-based, modern approach which includes technology and economic growth (albeit reformulated)?

The progression left to right in the boxes is from – laagers and lifeboats (top left and bottom left), through changed values and behaviour change – voluntary simplicity (top centre) and live close to the land (bottom centre) – to 'green after gold' (top right) where innovation and economic growth enable problems to be solved. Geo-engineering might exemplify this 'we are in charge and we can fix it' theme.

Bottom right in the red box would fit the logic of the circular economy: changed worldview, working with the flow, decoupling as well as redefining the value creation mechanisms, and their relationship to materials. Shifting to renewables. We are not in charge but we do have influence.

To return to the example in the schooling setting and given the emphasis on behaviour and values, it's hard to expect discussion to be elsewhere on this grid. There is little 'room' for it. But to get to a basic circular economy (bottom centre) for all, by assuming away modernity, seems a massive price to pay to maintain even a foothold on moral high ground. Choose less and/or live differently. Some choice, and that just for the committed. It probably won't work except as a niche solution. It is hard to think that young people would go for either. Why should they? In a basically unreformed linear economy, reducing total consumption boomerangs on the economy and in that boomerang the political legitimacy of the simpler life simply dissolves.

Young consumers out on the town

The puzzle must be that individual responsibility and guilt are weapons deployed in ostensibly economic discussions at all. They feel like a reaction against modernity of the most irrational sort. An exercise in feeling better, perhaps? If the context were a post-carbon crash, then it's an end to modernity anyway. It would be hard to imagine pre-industrial methods feeding existing urban world populations or holding up the infrastructure.

Instead, the educational discussion needs to be broad and it needs to include the systemic. It is the system conditions we choose which may be the key to either transitioning to a circular economy for an urban, populous and modern world or a much diminished economy built, by default, on the 'best of the rest' – what we can get from continuing a linear mode and trusting to technology and innovation. Standing back a little, it is easy to see planned obsolescence and an endless parade of cheap novelty as outcomes of that aggregation of choices over the years that we label the linear economy.

Perhaps no moral high ground is needed, merely an observation that were system conditions changed, by intention or circumstance, there would be an organic and adaptive shift in behaviour, as people adjusted to a different pattern of opportunities and incentives.

Understanding the 'bigger picture', seeing the connections and context, will remain a prerequisite of success but that context is now much wider. The fittest will be those who fit the system best, not those who aim to be last man or woman standing. To that degree, if the empathetic circuitry in the brain, the sense of other and context, is as important as cognitive science reports that it is (see opposite page) – every bit as important as the competitive, egocentric and individualistic drive – then what will result is the chance of a more cognitively balanced individual.

Being in favour of more cognitively rounded individuals in a restorative economy could be described as taking a position about what is right and good. So maybe we are stuck with morals somewhere but at least the focus is shifted outwards – from 'what is good for me and mine' to 'what is good for us and also me?' Please note the question mark.

The way to start, if we are talking education and particularly schools, is surely not to assume it is always (or even mostly) about changing individual behaviour in the frame of a moral or health programme – 'wash your hands, dear, and pick up that litter'. Instead it needs to be an education which, as the name suggests, draws out or opens up a world of possibilities, to see the world through different frames and to focus its attention as much on the context and the bigger picture, its connections and flow as it now spends on knowledge, detail and utility/vocation (or to be less generous – getting a good job).

Out of this kind of dynamic tension comes creativity just as it leads to innovation in the economy. A circular economy reflected in education is thus part of the search for a way of reinventing progress, to be a part of 21st-century Enlightenment in line with our evolving understanding of science and learning and of the interplay between the economy and its contexts.

HOW WE THINK AND HOW WE LEARN

The way we think is undoubtedly a crucial starting point. Cognitive scientists George Lakoff and Mark Johnson's work[4] on metaphor looks productive. They claim that cognitive science points to most thought being unconscious and that abstract thought is largely metaphorical. We do not see the world as it is but interpret it through frameworks which reflect 'worldviews.' These world views as the name suggests are based on metaphor, groupings of reinforcing metaphors which create a framework. Do we see the world as 'machine-like' or as a given Divine order, or 'random', or as a dynamic self-regulating system: do we see the nation as a family and what kind of family – one which is strict and hierarchical, or more inclusive and nurturing? The wash-up is that changing one's mind means being willing to engage with another framework or at least to use it more often. This then has many spin-offs. It suggests that just rehearsing facts has little impact if the facts don't fit a framework. It suggests that we do not make up our own mind, and that understanding one's own values, as they are represented through a worldview, is crucial. *And in education it means that context matters.* The idea of neutral knowledge transmission or contextless skills development is false: knowledge and skills will always and forever be embedded in some framework or other. As an approach, Lakoff and Johnson's work is called embodied realism. It also points to arch designer and provocateur Buckminster Fuller being on the mark when he said:

"You never change things by fighting the existing reality. To change something, build a new model that makes the existing model obsolete."

And on a related theme...

"If you want to teach people a new way of thinking, don't bother trying to teach them. Instead, give them a tool, the use of which will lead to new ways of thinking."

FROM THIS:

**1. DEVELOP LEARNER'S INSIGHTS
ON HOW NATURE WORKS**

**2. DEVELOP LEARNER'S INSIGHTS ON HOW
'CRADLE TO CRADLE' DESIGN AND THE 'CIRCULAR ECONOMY'
WORK c.f. A LINEAR ECONOMY**

**3. DEVELOP LEARNER'S INSIGHTS ABOUT
1 AND 2 USING INNOVATIVE PARTICIPATIVE
LEARNING APPROACHES**

TO THIS:

**1, 2 AND 3 SHARE THE SAME SYSTEMS THINKING -
USING 'CLOSED LOOPS' AND 'FEEDBACK'**

Source: Ken Webster and Craig Johnson, Sense and Sustainability (2010)

It's tempting to suggest that there is some new knowledge needed here, or rather knowledge that students don't usually encounter. True enough, so that would be 'content'... It's clear that there is something about participative learning too, with our keen interest in the role of feedback, so 'skills' then.

Add in some explorations about bringing this together so it gets around the trap of specialisms and siloing of knowledge, and that is a programme and a half of work already.

Recent studies by educationalists Bill Lucas and Guy Claxton seem in tune with this changing world. They advocate 'reframing discussion on skills in terms of developing dispositions and habits of mind'.[5] This connects with the thinking of Howard Gardner around 'multiple intelligences' and our learning preferences. It also connects with leading intellectual and business advisor Nassim Taleb who writes: 'Solutions can only come from simple heuristics. That's what we have been doing since civilisation began ...' The underlying sense in the term 'circular economy' is an attempt at such a heuristic, a framework for thinking about resources and our relationship to them.

The education system, if it remains true to the rationale of mirroring the scientific state of play and the economic concerns of dominant nation-states and leading institutions within them, will want to evolve to enable learners to grasp the 'habits of mind', the 'simple heuristics' and the 'dispositions' that enable effective 'whole systems' design. Why? Because then the evolved education system reflects the economic advantages of the approach and as a consequence has utility. This spans systems, products, technologies, molecules, materials and energy flows, and perhaps makes explicit those links between the subject specialties that are chronically underplayed at the present time.

However, if schooling is a reflection of a machine age, the influence of which is still prevalent in today's world, it is doing its work rather badly – generating vast quantities of waste in the form of the underqualified and uninterested as well as the overqualified and frustrated. The challenge is that we now need creativity and its precursor, imagination, coupled to commitment and passion.

In any event, to reference back to the world of consumerist disengagement and distraction, education needs to help young people find meaning in what they do. Whether it can afford, let alone justify, doing this through large institutional arrangements conceived in Victorian times and now at the tail end of an era of cheap energy remains to be seen. Perhaps it will be found in informal channels, or truly novel educational arrangements.

What is important is that we do not imagine that the education which served the linear economy will serve us now with a couple of tweaks and new bells and whistles tagged on. It calls for the same creativity to match the demands that changing circumstances are and will be making on business and industry. Within whatever arrangement emerges, there is likely to be rebalancing, one which does not lose the importance of specialism and analysis and the detail but, like the idea of a mechanical, linear world, this has become a special case – the general case is firmly in the non-linear and systems arena.

The chart on page 189 summarises some of the dimensions of education and training that need to be rebalanced. It will look familiar as it has the same roots as the tables on pages 68 and 69. The headings in the left-hand column characterise the main approaches of the 20th century. The right-hand column indicates the directions in which we need to travel if we are to develop the innovative and adaptable school leaver who is able to acquire new 'habits of mind'.

Systems thinking emphasises that skills have to be broadly understood. Even something as laudable as 'problem solving' carries with it an assumption that a problem is capable of being fixed. This can be true but often it is not: problem contextualizing and intervention might be more appropriate: looking for the systems and how to adjust system conditions.

EXAMPLES OF REBALANCING TEACHING AND LEARNING

In dynamic systems, there is no fix, just intervention and review, an iterative process. As a consequence, since most real-life problems are contingent, 'solving' them is much more likely to be a cross-disciplinary effort – in business it would be decision-making units working as a team. In teaching and learning, the emphasis would be on opportunities for participatory learning and creative and critical thinking, above all.

To finish here is a short summary from the Ellen MacArthur Foundation's contribution to an Aldersgate Group report[6] which reflected on the kinds of skills needed for the future. The chapter is Leadership for a Circular Economy:

"Below we lay out our future vision as to what skills development will look like as we move towards a circular economy, to ensure the leaders of the future are skilled appropriately. We need to support the learners of today to become:

Systems thinkers – At present much learning and training is specialist. Whilst specialist knowledge and technical skills will always be important it is essential to see the wood for the trees. Systems thinking at all levels enables people to take a broad, holistic view thus enabling them to make connections and see possibilities, to adapt in response to feedback.

Pro-active, independent enquirers – Small children are naturally inquisitive. As they progress through formal education and training this curiosity is burnished and encouraged. Learners and their teachers are rewarded for taking risks, for exploring issues from different perspectives, for making reasoned judgements.

Self-managers – Learners organise their own time, establish their own priorities and are able and willing to change in the light of feedback. They look actively for fresh opportunities, and manage their own learning to be able to rise to new challenges.

REBALANCING THE SKILLS MIX

20th century	21st century
Problem solving	Problem appreciation and reframing
Analysis	Synthesis
Reductionism	Whole system emphasis
Closed and immediate cause and effect	Multiple influences through time and space
Individual learning	Team or group learning
Being competitive	Competitive and collaborative
Emphasis on teacher transmitting predetermined knowledge to the student	Learning through enquiry with appropriate mentoring
Rooted in subjects or disciplines	Meta-learning

Creative innovators – No one has the monopoly of wisdom. As we explore the era post cheap oil and materials with its new and challenging predicaments, education and training aim to develop creative people who can reframe the way we think, come up with novel ways of optimising systems and creating multiple benefits for a wide range of stakeholders including those as yet unborn.

Team workers, effective participators and empathetic colleagues – People are social beings and formal education empowers learners to be empathetic, to respect the views of others and to contribute their own views, knowledge and skills clearly and with confidence. For this they need mastery of language and mathematics. They are able to work collaboratively and resolve disputes in which they are themselves a party.

Reflective practitioners committed to lifelong learning – Systems without feedback are stupid, by definition, so feedback loops are essential to all meaningful learning. Learners develop the habits of self-monitoring and reflection, listening to and offering constructive criticism, and making changes. This never stops and formal education feeds into the greater project: lifelong learning."

Photo: Thinkstock

11 CONCLUSION – RECOVERING REASON

Iteration. Complex systems rise, maintain themselves or fall through iteration. Feedback rules. It is time, now the end of this book is in sight, to look forward to the next iteration by first, looking back. As we know, the basics of a circular economy are decades old at least, if conceived of as an economy which might enable us to become 'at home in the modern world'. It is not a rejection of industrialisation – far from it – but a reconnection and a recontextualisation of it. John Lyle wrote cogently on this many years ago when he made the distinction between what he called 'degenerative and regenerative economies':

"Industrial systems are the products of recent western technology in its purest form, shaped by engineering criteria that seek high levels of productivity and operational efficiency to the virtual exclusion of other concerns. Therein lies their utility and occasional grandiose beauty – and their incipient failure.

Regenerative systems by contrast are enmeshed in natural and social processes in ways that make their purpose far more complex. While technology remains the means for augmenting nature, it ideally becomes a factor within the larger social and ecological context rather than the engine driving that complex.

Furthermore, with the need to interrelate technology with society and nature a broad and disparate knowledge enters the process."[1]

Resilience

" I can't understand why people are frightened of new ideas. I'm frightened of the old ones "
John Cage, musician

In this book the case is made that a circular economy has its roots in the updating of our scientific understanding, to acknowledge ordered complexity as the heart of almost all real world systems and relocate the linear system as a limited case, not the general case. John Lyle's 'broad and disparate knowledge' enters the process and speaks to new 'habits of thought' that are orientated towards systems thinking with its big picture, longer term, pattern-seeking concerns.

Although John Lyle and Joël de Rosnay, for example, locate the systems thinking revolution in the advent of computer modelling at MIT after World War 2 it is significant that in many respects it has been very slow progress. Even after a flurry of interest in business circles in the mid-1990s – paralleling the rise of complexity science after the desktop computing revolution of the period – interest has subsided through to the present day, gone underground or to the 'geeks'. It is much the same in education pre-19 where creative and critical thinking – associated with the higher order skills of analysis, evaluation, synthesis – once a widespread aspiration in better-funded times is now more talked about than evidenced.

In times of uncertainty there is always a tendency to conservatism and fundamentalism. It never works for long: Jericho's walls crumble, from their own internal failings. This book has supported the argument that it is in these times of uncertainty that the higher order skills, in context – the circular economy is one example of a context – are evidently *most* valuable to a society, as it tries to remake itself.

BUT WHEN WILL THE TRUMPETS SOUND?

It is unusual and disturbing to be living in an age where the merits or otherwise of a shift from linear to non-linear science seem to be located somewhere between Cloud 9 and Planet Irrelevance. Even Science (big S) is less and less the arbiter of what is thought generally 'reasonable', whether as a guide to policy or popular sentiment. Part of the problem was in science itself; it allowed the populace to believe it held the power to predict and control rather than just *explain*. When prediction and control came unstuck so did some of science's credibility. Science is often treated with suspicion or even roundly ignored in preference to opinion and prejudice with very little remaining in the way of general social sanction. Where once we looked to experts – and grumbled at their patronising manner – we now have blogs and Twitter to amplify the noise from the street. It's the persistent tinnitus of modern life. Instead of being a laughing stock the unreasonable becomes acceptable by repetition and punditry. A society made to believe it is composed of self-interested sovereign consumers soon assumes that deciding the merits of the mumps, measles and rubella (MMR) vaccine, or what a changing climate entails, is as much within their remit and right as what to have on a family meal out. It is a great sadness, as designer Buckminster Fuller remarked:

"I'm not trying to counsel any of you to do anything really special except dare to think. And to dare to go with the truth. And to dare to really love completely."

Doing none of the above has become the default in a more fearful, less confident society.

What is perhaps so very interesting is the coming together of so many forces and factors at this time: enlightened self-interest in manufacturing circles; the progress towards an ever more devolved economy – while acknowledging the growth of just a few very large firms; the power to spread open source, crowd funded ideas in the social media; the educational opportunities, especially for the autodidact; and the shift amongst the young towards valuing experience rather than ownership. Lastly, the confidence of science in the reality of ordered complexity and the iterative non-linear system is becoming the lens for all our serious thought on the issues of the day, or so we would no doubt wish.

But a lesson from history. Expect the unexpected. Change in iterative systems can be very sudden, and full of unforeseen consequences.

Anyone who promises that a circular economy will fix the ills of the world is at least misinformed. It is part of the understanding of systems as non-linear systems that no one should be foolish enough to predict the outcome, let alone guarantee it. But this does not mean we can say nothing, that the outcome is near to a random walk through the possibilities. It is, rather, a system open to influence, open to a degree of explanation and representation and to modelling.

The decision societies will come to make, if democracy survives or thrives, will be around setting the rules of the game to enable positive flows and watching the system iterate, and adjusting the rules as experience reveals. After all, if we have abandoned fundamentalism as irrational, and mechanistic control as naïve, what else can we do?

At the beginning of the book, the early summary of a circular economy made a play for the role of active citizens in a thriving democracy. According to economist Herman Daly, abundance and excess capacity is a prerequisite for freedom and democracy. Scarcity and the struggle for resources breed authoritarianism. He warns of working right up to the limits of natural capital, even if we could:

> **Excess carrying capacity is a necessary condition for freedom and democracy. Living close to the limit of carrying capacity, as on a submarine or spaceship, requires very strict discipline. On submarines we have a captain with absolute authority, not a democracy. If we want democracy, we better not grow up to the limit of carrying capacity — better to leave some slack, some margin for tolerance of the disagreements and errors that freedom entails.**
>
> **The more obvious political cost of growth is war for access to rival resources — minerals, water, agricultural land, and the remaining commons. The hope that economic growth would mean ever more things for ever more people, and would therefore keep the hounds of war at bay, may have been temporarily credible in yesterday's empty world, but not in today's full world.[2]**

There are a number of tensions here: a circular economy operated at the limits might be just so complex as to be unmanageable within an acceptable political system, one which might breed conflict and perhaps 'uneconomic growth' (costs greater than benefits) in its place. Yet if Amory Lovins is right, there is so much slack in the economy, so much waste, so much depleted capital that could be rebuilt, that the danger of running to the notional limits is small – at least for now. And if we think very differently, not least about what growth means and how it works out for the wider polity... Here is Nick Hanauer on growth:

"Prosperity in human societies can't be properly understood by just looking at monetary measures of income or wealth. Prosperity in a society is *the accumulation of solutions to human problems.*
These solutions run from the prosaic, like a crunchier potato chip, to the profound, like cures for deadly diseases. Ultimately, the measure of a society's wealth is the range of human problems that it has found a way to solve and how available it has made those solutions to its citizens."[3]

Amory Lovins is a great thinker in the rational tradition but many of his ideas require an appreciation of systems, complexity and how important it might be to rethink even existing infrastructure – for example, shifting centralized electrical grids to decentralized renewable-based systems.

An informed citizenry is required and one relaxed enough and prosperous enough to want to explore the new, to try some things out via private business or public investment (as with most infrastructure). Instead, as we have seen, an increasingly hollowed-out middle class in the 34 OECD countries is struggling to hold on to the advantages gained in an era of linear economics (characterized by cheap energy, materials and available credit) and is often wary of science and 'ideas' in general. In an era of jobless growth, conformity and emotional bonds pay more dividends. As well as a struggling middle class there is a casualised labour force with even less of a toehold in the system – with little time, opportunity or inclination to explore new ideas.

In the developing nations there are other more immediate challenges around water, food, pollution, energy and 'over-development' as evidenced by the underwriting of a credit-fueled building boom in China, leading to swathes of unoccupied apartments and offices.

What prospects then for circularity? In a stubbornly irrational world where scarcity, indebtedness and lack of opportunity are assumed and power wielded accordingly, there would be little to say. It would instead be a kind of business as usual, with better material flows but in essence the rump of the linear economy and for the majority a continuing, if

Restorative technologies – at least when combined. Part of the Sahara Forest Project
Image: saharaforestproject.com

❝ If we could learn to make things and do things the way nature does, we could achieve factor 10, factor 100, maybe even factor 1,000 savings in resource and energy use. ❞

Michael Pawlyn, Director,
The Sahara Forest Project

uneven, decline in living standards punctuated by credit-induced asset bubbles and shrinking public services. But as part of a new wave of enlightenment – 21st century Enlightenment – the circularity narrative could bring a widespread prosperity by simply outcompeting the old. The key to such Enlightenment is again, like Enlightenment 1.0, scientific but it is around the better understanding which accompanies a systems perspective. The wealth of flows. The wealth inherent in flows derived from and reinforcing the capitals, economic, social and natural. Effective flows which enable business and communities at all scales to create income not just obtain cheaper goods as the fruits of efficiency. A simple reminder that it is the customer who creates wealth and to do that they need income.

Systems thinking is key to the circular economy: part of the solution is education and training. The Centre for a Circular Economy, based at Bradford University's re:centre, opened in 2014.
Photo: Craig Johnson

To be truly disruptive the acceleration of the transition towards a circular economy encompasses the logic of a systems perspective and works as well at the micro as well as at the macro scale. It is a nested (fractal) arrangement after all. If combined, the strands of a devolved (empowering) and sharing (social capital building) economy, collaborative use and new kinds of abundance from circularity (effective materials and energy flows) can fuel the interests of the winners to push for revised 'rules of the game' (tax shifting) to create a new and truly level playing field. Further capitalisation on knowledge to find progressively more nuanced and elegant solutions will accelerate change in a positive cycle. It's all of the above, synergistically related which makes the difference. It has other benefits too.

"The accepted ideas of any period are singularly those that serve the dominant economic interest ... Not to notice this takes effort, although many succeed."
J K Galbraith, The Age Of Uncertainty

With rising incomes and more widespread economic participation comes a revival in democratic processes and the valuing of scientifically based debate. People do value results. The use of the science of complexity – to provide the rationale which enables optimised systems, multiplied cash flows, cascaded materials and closed loops – will be acknowledged as the roots of how enduring economic prosperity can be delivered. With that broad spectrum success, the new business, social and political leaderships who gain from it then enshrine and entrain these ideas in new iterations of the education system, economics, culture and technology just as surely as the beneficiaries of the ideas of an earlier Enlightenment did two hundred years ago ... because they worked.

A REGENERATIVE CIRCULAR ECONOMY

can be seen as the effective flow of materials, energy and information in relation to maintenance or increase of stocks of capital: ECONOMIC, SOCIAL, HUMAN AND NATURAL.

- It uses insights from the functioning of non-linear systems – feedback-rich systems, and especially living systems – as a framework for thinking.

- Its study is likely to have in mind nested systems (fractal scale, diverse periodicities) with histories and entrainment but also emergent properties and the possibility of evolution.

- Characterisation: the bigger picture, the longer term and by intention (design).

WASTE = FOOD
SHIFT > RENEWABLES
PRICES = FULL COSTS
MONEY = MEDIUM OF EXCHANGE
DIVERSITY = STRENGTH

- The circular economy can be explored through a number of identities and one related shift. In a circular (feedback-rich) system the endless transformation means that one side of the equation has an intimate relationship with the other if it is to 'work' optimally as a system.

- Using the three categories of materials, energy and information and informed by systems thinking, the four identities fall into place.

Materials flows are ideally in either biological or technical cycles

MATERIALS →

WASTE = FOOD BIOLOGICAL
- This is a consumer pathway
- Biological materials cascade
- Value is extracted in stages towards the final decomposition and reuse in the system.
- Eliminate toxics.

MATERIALS →

WASTE = FOOD TECHNICAL
- This is a user pathway.
- Technical materials can cascade
- Value is related to maintenance of quality and embedded energy for defined use periods.
- Upcycling (adding quality or upgrading) is possible with sufficient surplus energy

ENERGY →

SHIFT > RENEWABLES
- A progressive shift towards renewables over time,
- Assisted by lowered energy thresholds via the impacts of better design and remarketing, reuse, refurbishment, repair and remanufacturing and the continuing fall in price for renewables.
- Use of current solar income not stored (i.e. fossil fuels)

INFORMATION →

PRICES = FULL COSTS
- Markets are effective arbiters of resource allocation when rational decision-making is possible.
- Prices are messages and therefore need to accurately reflect all costs.

INFORMATION →

MONEY = MEDIUM OF EXCHANGE
- Materials and service flows require appropriate and sufficient medium of exchange to be effective
- – includes complementary currencies.

INFORMATION →

DIVERSITY = STRENGTH
- A dynamic relationship between efficiency and resilience.
- The role of diversity in feedback–rich systems is to provide both resilience and innovation (creativity and its application) in response to change.

Sources: Synthesised by Ken Webster from McDonough and Braungart, Stahel, Lovins, Hawken, Anderson, Holling, Boulding, Webster and Fuller.

201

NOTES AND REFERENCES

INTRODUCTION

1 Paul Ormerod, *Butterfly Economics, A New General Theory of Social and Economic Behaviour* (Basic Books, 1998).
2 Eric Beinhocker, *The Origin of Wealth: Evolution, Complexity and the Radical Remaking of Economics* (Random House, 2007).
3 Nick Hanauer and Eric Liu, *Gardens of Democracy: A New American Story of Citizenship, the Economy, and the Role of Government* (Sasquatch Books, 2011).
4 Amory Lovins, *Reinventing Fire* http://www.rmi.org/ReinventingFire
5 see http://www.natcap.org/images/other/NCsynopsis.pdf
6 From the Preface to Amory Lovins, Hunter Lovins and Paul Hawken, *Natural Capitalism* (Earthscan, 1999).
7 http://www.c2ccertified.org/
8 Hanauer and Liu, op. cit.

CHAPTER 1 ALL THE FLOWS, HISTORY TOO

1 http://journal.frontiersin.org/Journal/10.3389/fenrg.2013.00009/full
2 http://www.unccd.int/en/media-center/Press-Releases/Pages/Press-Release-Detail.aspx?PRId=44
3 New Scientist, *All together now and picking up pace?* (2008).
4 *Bankrupting Nature,* by Anders Wijkman and Johan Rockström, *The Future* by Al Gore, and the Worldwatch Institute series *State of the World* and *Vital Signs* http://www.worldwatch.org/
5 http://www.gmo.com/websitecontent/GMO_QtlyLetter_ALL_4Q2013.pdf
6 http://uk.businessinsider.com/jeremy-grantham-on-oil-economic-growth-2014-11
7 A new oil strike can be a 'gusher', requiring little additional energy to produce the oil – a ratio of 100:1 indicates 1 barrel of oil is required to extract 100 barrels of oil. But as the oil field ages it will require more and more effort to pump the remaining oil out.
8 http://www.washingtonpost.com/blogs/wonkblog/wp/2013/04/13/peak-oil-isnt-dead-an-interview-with-chris-nelder/April 13
9 James Murray and Jim Hansen, *Peak Oil and Energy Independence: Myth and Reality* EOS (Vol 94, Issue 28, 9/7/2013), pp.245–246.
see also Nafeez Ahmed (Institute for Policy Research and Development) in http://www.guardian.co.uk/environment/earth-insight/2013/jul/23/peak-oil-bbc-shale-fracking-economy-recession

CHAPTER 2 THE NECESSITY OF A CIRCULAR ECONOMY?

1 *Global overproduction will hinder plastics industry growth* (Central News Agency Taiwan, 15-11-2011) http://www.taiwannews.com.tw/etn/news_content.php?id=1759566.
2 http://www.zo2.ch/fr/index.php/research/games/
3 Complexity theory:
http://www2.econ.iastate.edu/tesfatsi/RethinkingEconomicsUsingComplexityTheory.DHelbingAKirman2013.pdf
4 Goerner, S., Dyck, R. and Lagerroos, D. *The New Science of Sustainability: Building a Foundation for Great Change* (Chapel Hill, NC: Triangle Center for Complex Systems, distributed by Gabriola Island, BC, Canada: New Society Publishers 2009).
5 George Lakoff and Mark Johnson, *Philosophy in the Flesh: The Embodied Mind and Its Challenge to Western Thought* (Basic Books, 1999).

CHAPTER 3 FROM LINEAR TO CIRCULAR (none)

CHAPTER 4 THROUGH THE MACROSCOPE

1 Joël de Rosnay, *The Macroscope* (Harper Row, New York, 1979). Available online http://pespmc1.vub.ac.be/macrbook.html
2 On that topic applied to the economy, Stahel and Giarini's book *The limits to certainty* (2nd revised edition, Kluwer Academic Publishers, 1993) provides useful insights.
3 E P Odum and H T Odum, *Fundamentals of Ecology* (Saunders, 1953).
4 Nationwide Mutual Insurance Company (US) http://www.youtube.com/watch?v=8qD6RWIDeuY
5 Andy Haldane, *Rethinking the Financial Network* Speech delivered at the Financial Student Association in Amsterdam, 28 April 2009.
6 Bela H. Benathy, *Systems Design of Education: A Journey to Create the Future* (Educational Technology Publications 1991).
7 From Gary Swift, *Anatomy of a Pattern Language* DesignMatriX http://www.designmatrix.com/pl/anatomy.html

CHAPTER 5 CONSUMER TO USER (none)

CHAPTER 6 SOCIAL CAPITAL, MARKETS AND MONEY IN A CIRCULAR ECONOMY

1 Richard Dobbs et al., *Resource Revolution: Meeting the world's energy, materials, food and water needs* (McKinsey Global Institute).
2 http://torekes.be/
3 http://www.collaborativefinance.org/mutual-credit/complementary-currencies/
4 http://www.thepaypers.com/mobile-payments/60-of-kenyans-use-their-mobile-phone-for-banking-transactions-report/753856-16
5 http://intrastructures.net/Intrastructures/Actions_-_mobilotoop.html also http://www.flandersinshape.be/frontend/files/userfiles/files/MOBILOTOOP%20 PUBLICATIE-small.pdf
6 http://www.doorsofperception.com/notopic/caloryville-the-two-wheeled-city/#more-5866
7 See more at: http://www.doorsofperception.com/notopic/caloryville-the-two-wheeled-city/
8 Michael Lind, *Land of Promise: An Economic History of the United States* (Harper 2012), available online: http://www.salon.com/2013/03/21/private_sector_parasites/

CHAPTER 7 THE SHARING ECONOMY

1 http://www.mongabay.com/commodities/prices/average-petroleum-price.php
2 http://www.mongabay.com/commodities/prices/copper.php
3 http://minerals.usgs.gov/minerals/pubs/commodity/indium/indiumyb05.pdf
4 http://www.eia.gov/coal/review/pdf/feature05.pdf
5 http://www.rolls-royce.com/news/press-releases/yr-2012/121030-the-hour.aspx
6 http://www.economist.com/news/leaders/21573104-internet-everything-hire-rise-sharing-economy

CHAPTER 8 DEVOLVED, DIGITAL AND OPEN-SOURCE MANUFACTURING AND THE RISE OF URBAN MINING

1 http://www.ellenmacarthurfoundation.org/blog/project-mainstream
2 Janine Benyus, *Biomimicry: Innovation Inspired by Nature* (William Morow, 2nd edition, 2002).
3 Adapted from Mark Boyer, *Biomimicry is the Key to a Green 3D Printing Revolution*, (06/22/13) http://inhabitat.com/biomimicry-3-8-founder-janine-benyus-says-biomimicry-is-the-key-to-a-green-3d-printing-revolution/
4 http://www.ifixit.com
5 http://opensourceecology.org/gvcs/

6 Thomas E Graedel, 'The Prospects for Urban Mining' in *The Bridge* (No1 Vol 41 2011) http://www.nae.edu/Publications/Bridge/43180/47182.aspx

7 According to the US Environmental Protection Agency (EPA), "One metric ton of circuit boards can contain 40 to 800 times the concentrations of gold ore mined in the US and 30–40 times the concentration of copper ore mined in the US." http://www.epa.gov/epawaste/conserve/materials/ecycling/faq.htm

8 "Today, approximately 75% of all the aluminium ever produced is still in productive use, having been through countless loops of its lifecycle," says Ken Martchek, International Aluminium Institute Energy and Environment Committee Chairman.

9 http://www.gunterpauli.com/Gunter_Pauli/Blog/Entries/2013/6/6_Reindustrialization_beyond_Globalization.html

CHAPTER 9 THE REGENERATIVE BIOLOGICAL CYCLE – AT SCALE

1 See *Towards the Circular Economy: Vol 2,* pp.17–24, as a reminder of the existing pluses and minuses of the agricultural system operating on a large scale.

2 Ibid p.21.

3 Ibid p.22.

4 www.savoryinstitute.com

5 http://www.wired.co.uk/magazine/archive/2013/08/features/post-organic

6 F Kirschenmann, *The current state of agriculture. Does it have a future?* in N. Wirzba (ed.), *The future of culture, community and the land* (University Press of Kentucky 2003).

7 Mae Wan Ho, *One bird – ten thousand treasures. How the duck in the paddy fields can feed the world* (Paper published at the Institute of Science in Society (ISIS) website, 1999).

8 Kirschenmann, ibid

9 Duck-rice film featuring Takeo Furono, https://www.youtube.com/watch?v=pqpEg45fp4I

CHAPTER 10 EDUCATION IN A CHANGING WORLD

1 The Futuretrack report, undertaken by the Institute for Employment Research at the University of Warwick, reported here http://www.thecompleteuniversityguide.co.uk/news/forty-percent-of-grads-in-non-grad-jobs,-says-report/

2 http://usatoday30.usatoday.com/money/perfi/college/story/2011-10-19/student-loan-debt/50818676/1

3 Thomas Berry, 'The New Story', *Teilhard Studies #1* (Anima Press, American Teilhard Association, Winter 1978).

4 George Lakoff and Mark Johnson, *Philosophy in the Flesh: The Embodied Mind and Its Challenge to Western Thought* (Basic Books, 1999).

5 Bill Lucas and Guy Claxton, *Wider skills for learning* (Centre for Real World Learning and NESTA, 2009).

6 Andrew Raingold, *Skills for a New Economy: A paradigm shift in education and learning to ensure future economic success* (The Aldersgate Group, October 2012), available online: http://www.aldersgategroup.org.uk/reports

CHAPTER 11 CONCLUSION: RECOVERING REASON

1 John T Lyle, *Regenerative Design for Sustainable Development* (Wiley, 1996), Chapter 3.

2 Herman Daly, *Growth And Laissez-faire* 01 October, 2013 http://www.countercurrents.org/daly011013.htm

3 Nick Hanauer and Eric Liu, *Gardens of Democracy* (Sasquatch Books, 2011).

SOME INTERESTING READING

SYSTEMS
Donella H Meadows, *Thinking in Systems* (Chelsea Green, 2008)
Kenneth M Stokes, *Man and the Biosphere* (M E Sharpe, 1994)
Christopher Alexander et al., *A Pattern Language* (Oxford University Press, 1977)
Joël de Rosnay, *The Macroscope* (Harper Row, 1979), available online http://pespmc1.vub.ac.be/macrbook.html

DESIGN
William McDonough and Michael Braungart, *Cradle to Cradle: Remaking the Way We Make Things* (North Point Press, 2002)
William McDonough and Michael Braungart, *The Upcycle: Beyond Sustainability – Designing for Abundance* (2014)
Janine Benyus, *Biomimicry: Innovation Inspired by Nature* (William Morow, 2nd edition, 2002)
Michael Pawlyn, *Biomimicry in Architecture* (RIBA Publishing, 2011)
Lloyd Steven Sieden, *Buckminster Fuller's Universe: His Life and Work* (Basic Books, 2000)

ENERGY
Amory Lovins & Rocky Mountain Institute, *Reinventing Fire* (Chelsea Green, 2011)
Howard T Odum, *Environment, Power and Society for the 21st Century* (Columbia University Press, 2007)

ECONOMICS AND BUSINESS
Gunter Pauli, *The Blue Economy* (Paradigm Publications, 2010)
Walter Stahel, *The Performance Economy* (Palgrave Macmillan, 2010)
Amory Lovins, Hunter Lovins and Paul Hawken, *Natural Capitalism* (Earthscan, 1999)

THE ELLEN MACARTHUR FOUNDATION

MISSION
TO ACCELERATE THE TRANSITION
TO A CIRCULAR ECONOMY

The Foundation works across three interlinking areas:

EDUCATION
INSPIRING A GENERATION
TO RE-THINK THE FUTURE

Inspiring and enabling learners to apply contemporary science (systems thinking) to the challenge of building a circular economy and reflecting this opportunity to their lives, skills and futures. By leveraging the power of online learning to connect people and break down educational barriers across the world, the Foundation is creating a global teaching and learning platform built around the circular economy framework. With an emphasis on online learning we aim to provide cutting edge insight and content to support circular economy education. This work runs alongside a Pioneer University Network and Fellowship Programme, focussing on fostering academic research and teaching with partners in Europe, the US, India, China and South America.

BUSINESS
CATALYSING CIRCULAR INNOVATION
ACROSS THE ECONOMY

Since its launch in September 2010, the Foundation has placed an emphasis on the real-world relevance of its activities. The Foundation understands that business innovation sits at the heart of any transition to the circular economy. The Foundation works with its Global Partners (Cisco, Philips, Renault, Unilever and Kingfisher) to address major challenges in accelerating the transition to the circular economy. In February 2013, with the support of its Global Partners, the Foundation created the world's first dedicated circular economy innovation programme. The Circular Economy 100 comprises a group of industry-leading corporations, emerging innovators (SMEs), cities, governments and pioneering universities. The programme provides a unique forum for businesses to build circular capabilities, address common barriers to progress and pilot circular practices in a collaborative environment.

ANALYSIS
ROBUST EVIDENCE ABOUT
THE BENEFITS OF THE TRANSITION

The Foundation works to quantify the economic potential of the circular model and develop approaches for capturing this value. Working together with its Knowledge Partner, McKinsey & Company, the Foundation has created a series of economic reports highlighting the rationale for an accelerated transition towards the circular economy. The Foundation believes the circular economy is an evolving framework and continues to widen its understanding by working with a network of international experts including key circular economy thinkers and leading academics. These external experts feed into the key programmes that we run as well as contributing to our growing body of reports, resources, case studies and publications.

www.ellenmacarthurfoundation.org